用英语讲中国好故事

成语故事

THE IDIOM STORIES

（汉英对照）

韩　进 ◎ 编著
司梦琪 ◎ 译

北京师范大学出版集团
BEIJING NORMAL UNIVERSITY PUBLISHING GROUP
安徽大学出版社

图书在版编目(CIP)数据

成语故事:汉英对照/韩进编著;司梦琪译. —合肥:安徽大学出版社,2021.4
(用英语讲中国好故事)
ISBN 978-7-5664-2210-1

Ⅰ.①成… Ⅱ.①韩… ②司… Ⅲ.①汉语－成语－故事－青少年读物－汉、英 Ⅳ.①H136.31－49

中国版本图书馆 CIP 数据核字(2021)第 045630 号

成语故事:汉英对照
CHENGYU GUSHI:HANYING DUIZHAO

韩　进 编著
司梦琪 译

出版发行：	北京师范大学出版集团
	安　徽　大　学　出　版　社
	(安徽省合肥市肥西路 3 号 邮编 230039)
	www.bnupg.com.cn
	www.ahupress.com.cn
印　　刷：	安徽省人民印刷有限公司
经　　销：	全国新华书店
开　　本：	170 mm×240 mm
印　　张：	13.5
字　　数：	214 千字
版　　次：	2021 年 4 月第 1 版
印　　次：	2021 年 4 月第 1 次印刷
定　　价：	39.00 元
ISBN 978-7-5664-2210-1	

策划编辑：李　梅　韦　玮　葛灵知　　　　装帧设计：丁　健
责任编辑：韦　玮　李　雪　　　　　　　　美术编辑：李　军
责任校对：高婷婷　　　　　　　　　　　　责任印制：赵明炎

版权所有　侵权必究

反盗版、侵权举报电话：0551—65106311
外埠邮购电话：0551—65107716
本书如有印装质量问题，请与印制管理部联系调换。
印制管理部电话：0551—65106311

前　言

　　青少年是在故事中成长的，听故事、读故事、讲故事，是他们的最爱。自古流传下来的故事浩如烟海，给他们挑选故事一定要慎之又慎，必须有益于身心健康，能够帮助他们扣好人生精神成长的第一粒扣子。

　　中华文化源远流长，在先贤留下的无数文化瑰宝中，神话、寓言、成语、童话和民间故事成为青少年必备的精神食粮，哺育他们成长，在薪火相传中延续中华文化的命脉。

　　每个民族都有自己的神话、寓言、成语、童话和民间故事，共同构成人类文化的宝库。中国的神话、寓言、成语、童话和民间故事蕴含着的中华文化，历来是世界了解中国的一扇窗户、一面镜子和一条捷径。

　　为弘扬中华文化，让更多海内外青少年更好地了解中华文化，我们编写了这套"用英语讲中国好故事"丛书。本丛书参照教育部统编语文教材推荐阅读书目的范围和要求，选取经过时间检验的神话、寓言、成语、童话和民间故事等经典篇目进行改编创作，在原汁原味讲述故事的同时，力求情节完整，语言流畅，读起来饶有趣味，又开卷有益。

　　在编排体例上，兼顾中外读者查询方便，以汉语拼音为序排列目录，中英文对照阅读，以清新活泼的风格亲近读者，满足其阅读期待。具体篇目一般从释义、故事、出处三部分进行解析，做到知识性、趣味性、教育性、可读性并重。在篇目选择和改编过程中，作者参阅了有关资料，注意汲取同类选本的编写经验，再根据本丛书读者的定位，进行有针对性地阅读辅导。故事虽然还是那些故事，但与现实的联系更加紧密了。

　　本丛书致力于让青少年读中华文化故事，推动中华文化"走出去"，构建人类精神家园。本丛书难免会有不足之处，欢迎读者批评指正，以期再版重印时加以修订完善。

韩　进

安徽省文艺评论家协会主席

2021 年 4 月 20 日

目 录
Contents

爱屋及乌 1
Love a Person and the Crow on His Roof 2
安步当车 4
Take Leisure Steps as a Ride 6
安居乐业 8
Live in Peace and Work Happily 9
按图索骥 11
Look for a Steed with Its Picture 12
百步穿杨 14
Shoot Willow Leaves a Hundred Steps away 16
杯弓蛇影 18
Mistake the Shadow of a Bow in the Cup as a Snake 19
鞭长莫及 21
Even a Long Whip Can't Reach It 22
不为五斗米折腰 24
Won't Bow for Five *Dou* of Rice 25
草木皆兵 27
Every Bushes and Trees Look like Enemies 28
程门立雪 31
The Snow Piles up at Cheng Yi's Door 32

寸阴尺璧 34
Time Is More Precious than Jade 35
道旁苦李 36
Bitter Plums by the Roadside 37
道听途说 39
Hear and Spread on the Road 41
东施效颦 43
Dongshi Imitates the Beauty 44
对牛弹琴 46
Play the *Guqin* to a Cow 47
多行不义必自毙 48
Evil Deeds Bring about Self-destruction 49
分道扬镳 51
Go Separate Ways 52
感恩图报 54
Feel Grateful and Plan to Repay It 55
观棋不语 57
Keep Silent While Watching the Chess Game 58
过门不入 60
Pass by the House Without Entering It 62
邯郸学步 65
Learn to Walk in Handan 66
狐假虎威 68
The Fox Exploits the Tiger's Might 69
画龙点睛 71
Add Eyes to a Dragon 72

画蛇添足 ... 74
Add Feet When Drawing a Snake ... 75
讳疾忌医 ... 77
Conceal the Illness from the Doctor ... 78
解铃还须系铃人 ... 80
Who Tied the Bell Should Untie It ... 81
惊弓之鸟 ... 83
A Bird Startled by a Bow ... 84
井底之蛙 ... 86
A Frog at the Bottom of a Well ... 87
九死一生 ... 89
A Narrow Escape from Death ... 90
开天辟地 ... 92
Split Heaven and Earth Apart ... 94
刻舟求剑 ... 96
Mark the Boat to Locate the Sword ... 97
滥竽充数 ... 99
Pretend to Play the *Yu* to Get by ... 100
老马识途 ... 102
An Old Horse Knows the Way ... 103
乐不思蜀 ... 105
So Happy as to Forget Shu ... 106
励精图治 ... 108
Arouse All Efforts to Make the Country Prosperous ... 109
两袖清风 ... 111
Two Sleeves of Breeze ... 112

柳暗花明	114
Beautiful Scene after the Dead End	115
毛遂自荐	118
Mao Sui Recommends Himself	119
名正言顺	121
Right Titles and Proper Words	122
磨杵成针	124
Grind an Iron Bar down to a Needle	125
南辕北辙	127
Go South by Driving Northward	128
呕心沥血	130
Spit out the Heart and Spill the Blood	131
披荆斩棘	133
Break Open a Way Through Thistles and Thorns	134
破釜沉舟	136
Break the Pots and Sink the Boats	137
七步之才	139
Seven-step Talent	140
杞人忧天	142
The Man of Qi State Worried That the Sky Would Fall	143
千里之堤,毁于蚁穴	145
A Thousand-mile Long Dam Can Be Destroyed by Ant Nests	146
前事不忘后事之师	148
The Past Is the Teacher of the Future	149
黔驴技穷	151
The Donkey of Qian Exhausted Its Tricks	152

穷兵黩武 154
Exhaust the Troops and Engage in Wars 155
曲高和寡 158
Difficult Songs Find Few Singers to Join in the Chorus 159
人琴俱亡 161
Both the Man and the *Guqin* Are Dead 162
人心如面 164
People's Hearts Are like Their Faces 165
任人唯贤 167
Appoint People by Their Merits 168
孺子可教 170
The Young Man Is Promising 171
入木三分 173
Written in a Forceful Hand 174
塞翁失马，焉知非福 176
Sai Weng's Lost of His Horse Maybe a Blessing in Disguise 177
三顾茅庐 179
Pay Three Visits to the Hut 180
三人成虎 182
Three Men's Talking Makes a Tiger 183
守株待兔 185
Guard a Tree-stump to Wait for Hares 186
熟能生巧 187
Practice Makes Perfect 188
揠苗助长 189
Pull up Seedlings to Help Them Grow 190

一夫当关，万夫莫开 192
One Man Can Hold out Against Ten Thousand 193
一馈十起 195
Rise Ten Times over a Meal 196
一目之罗 198
A One-mesh Net 199
朝三暮四 200
Three in the Morning and Four in the Evening 201
自相矛盾 203
Spear and Shield 204

爱屋及乌

【释义】爱一个人而连带爱他屋上停留的乌鸦。比喻爱一个人而连带喜爱与之有关的人或物。

【出处】《尚书大传·大战》："爱人者，兼其屋上之乌。"

传说商朝末年，纣王残暴不仁，引起民愤。西边有个叫周的诸侯国，其首领姬昌，后称为周文王，准备起兵东进，推翻纣王暴政，可惜壮志未酬就去世了。他的儿子姬发继位，即周武王，子承父志，联合各诸侯国出兵讨伐纣王，在牧野（今河南淇县西南）展开大战，大败纣王，攻入商朝首都，纣王自焚，商朝灭亡，西周王朝建立。

如何处置商朝遗留下来的旧部，稳定局面，武王心里没谱，忧心忡忡，于是征求军师姜子牙的意见。姜子牙说："我听说过这样的话，如果喜爱那个人，就连同他屋上的乌鸦也喜欢；如果不喜欢这个人，就连带厌恶他家的墙壁篱笆。"其意思是不能留下被俘虏的这些人。

武王认为不能这样，转而征求召公的意见。召公建议将有罪的人杀掉，无罪的人留下。武王也不以为然，继续征求周公的意见。周公建议让所有的俘虏都回到自己的家乡，耕种自己的田地，自食其力。武王认为周公的话有道理，就照此办理。武王以仁政感化天下，从此民心安定，西周也逐渐强大起来。

Love a Person and the Crow on His Roof

❀ Paraphrase

It is a **metaphor** that the love for somebody or something extends to everything related with it.

❀ Source

Great Wars, Shangshu Dazhuan: If you love someone, you will also love the crow on his roof.

It is said that in the last years of the Shang Dynasty, King Zhou was brutal and **inhumane**, causing people's anger. To the west, there was a vassal state called Zhou. Its leader Ji Chang, later known as King Wen of Zhou, prepared to march eastward and overthrow the tyranny of King Zhou. Unfortunately, he passed away without fulfilling his ambition. His son Ji Fa succeeded to the throne, that is, King Wu of Zhou. The son inherited his father's will, and joined the vassal states to send troops to defeat King Zhou, and launched a battle in Muye (now southwest of Qi county, Henan province), and defeated King Zhou. Invaded the capital of the Shang Dynasty, King Zhou set himself on fire. The Shang Dynasty was destroyed, and the Western Zhou Dynasty was established.

How to deal with the old ministry left over from the Shang Dynasty, and **stabilize** the situation, King Wu of

metaphor
n. 暗喻，隐喻

inhumane
adj. 不仁慈的，残忍的

stabilize
v. （使）稳定，稳固

Zhou didn't have a clue, so he asked his adviser Jiang Ziya for advice. Jiang Ziya said, "I've heard that if you like that person, you will also like the crow on his roof; if you don't like this person, you will even hate the walls and fences of his house." This meant that these prisoners could not be set at liberty.

King Wu didn't think that was a good idea, so he turned to Duke Zhao for advice. The duke suggested killing the guilty and leaving the innocent. King Wu did not agree and continued to pursue the opinion of Duke Zhou. Duke Zhou suggested that all the prisoners should return to their hometowns to till their own fields and earn their own living. King Wu thought Duke Zhou's words were reasonable and acted accordingly. King Wu influenced the world with his **benevolent** governance, and the people began to have a peaceful state of mind from then on, and the Western Zhou Dynasty gradually became stronger.

benevolent
adj. 仁慈的，慈善的

安步当车

【释义】以从容的步行代替乘车,形容轻松缓慢地行走。也指人能够安守贫贱生活。

【出处】《战国策·齐策四》:"晚食以当肉,安步以当车。"

战国时期,齐国有个叫颜斶的人,虽然很有才华,但他宁愿在家过着隐居生活,也不愿意做官。齐宣王爱惜他的才华,召他进宫。颜斶来到殿前,见宣王正等着他拜见,却停下了脚步,不再上前。

宣王说:"颜斶,请过来!"

颜斶说:"大王,请您过来!"

宣王听了很不高兴。大臣们纷纷质问颜斶:"大王是君主,你是臣民,大王可以叫你过来,你怎么可以叫大王过来呢?"颜斶不慌不忙地说:"话不能这么说。如果我走到大王面前,不免有巴结权势的嫌疑;如果是大王走过来,反而表明大王礼贤下士。"

宣王说:"到底是君王尊贵,还是士人尊贵?"

颜斶说:"当然是士人尊贵。"

宣王说:"有何依据?"

颜斶说:"从前秦国进攻齐国的时候,秦王曾下过一道命令:在柳下惠(春秋时期著名的贤士)坟墓周围五十步以内砍伐一草一木的,死!秦王进入齐国后,又下令:取齐王脑袋者,赏千金,封为万户侯。如此看来,一个活着的君主,还不如一个死了的士人坟墓周围的草木,请问君王和士人哪个尊贵?"

宣王说:"有才华的人真是得罪不起呀!从今往后,我拜你为师,遇事向你请教,请你住到我这里来,我们同享荣华富贵,你可愿意?"

颜斶说:"谢谢大王好意。我是个乡野之人,不习惯荣华富贵。我倒愿意'晚食以当肉,安步以当车,无罪以当贵,清净贞正以自娱'!"说完,转身就走。

颜斶的意思是:吃不起肉,可以把吃饭的时间推迟些,饿了吃饭,自然吃什么都香,就像吃肉一样;路走得安稳轻松,就像坐车一样舒服;不做坏事,清白正直,比当官发财还要高尚快乐。

Take Leisure Steps as a Ride

❖ Paraphrase

Walk leisurely instead of riding in a carriage. It also refers to the ability of people to live in poverty with enjoyment.

❖ Source

Strategies of Qi IV, Strategies of the Warring States: Take delayed meals as meat, and leisure steps as a ride.

During the Warring States Period, a man named Yan Chu in Qi State was very talented. He would rather live a **reclusive** life than be an official. King Xuan of Qi State **cherished** his talent and called him into the palace. Yan Chu came to the front of the hall and saw that King Xuan was waiting for him, but he stopped going forward.

King Xuan said, "Yan Chu, please come here!" Yan Chu said, "My king, please come here!"

King Xuan was very upset. The ministers questioned Yan Chu one after another, "The king is the king, and you are a subject. The king can call you over, but how can you call the king over?" Yan Chu said calmly, "That's wrong. If I walked to the king, there is **suspicion** of **fawning on** power; however, if the king comes to me, it will show that our king treats scholars with **courtesy**."

reclusive
adj. 隐居的，遁世的
cherish
v. 珍爱，爱护

suspicion
n. 嫌疑
fawn on
讨好，巴结
courtesy
n. 礼貌，彬彬有礼

King Xuan asked, "Is it the king or the scholar that is more honourable?" Yan Chu said, "Of course it is the scholar who is more honourable." King Xuan asked, "Why?"

Yan Chu said, "When Qin State attacked Qi State, King Qin once gave an order, 'Who cuts down a plant within 50 steps around the tomb of Liu Xiahui (a famous wise man in the Spring and Autumn Period) will be sentenced to death!' When King Qin entered Qi State, he gave another order, 'Those who take the head of King Qi will be rewarded with a large amount of gold, and the title of **marquis** of 10,000 households.' In this way, a living king is **inferior** to the plants around the grave of a dead scholar. May I ask which one is more honourable, the king or the scholar?"

King Xuan said, "I really can't afford to offend a talented person! From now on I will take you as my teacher and ask you for advice. Will you live with me, and let us enjoy the power and wealth together?"

Yan Chu said, "My king, thank you for your kindness. I am a countryman and I am not accustomed to **prosperity** and wealth. I would rather take delayed meals as meat, leisure steps as a ride, innocence as wealth, and integrity as entertainment!" Then he turned and walked away. Yan Chu's words mean: If you can't afford meat, you can put off your meal time. When you are hungry, everything tastes like meat; if you don't have a carriage, you can walk more calmly, and it's also comfortable; to be innocent and upright without doing anything bad is nobler and happier than to be an official and rich.

marquis
n. 侯爵

inferior
adj. 较差的，较次的

prosperity
n. 繁荣，兴旺

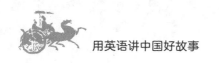

安居乐业

【释义】安定地生活，快乐地工作。

【出处】《老子》："民各甘其食，美其服，安其俗，乐其业，至老死不相往来。"

老子，春秋时期楚国人，是中国古代思想家、哲学家、文学家，道家学派创始人，代表作有《道德经》。

老子姓李名耳。关于老子姓名的由来，还有这样的传说。据说老子出生的时候，已经是满头白发，像个白胡子的小老头，所以人称"老子"。老子生下来就会说话，他指着院子中的一棵李子树说："李就是我的姓。"又因为他耳朵长得特别大，所以名"耳"。

老子生活在春秋战国时期，社会矛盾复杂，战争不断，生活极不稳定，老子非常眷恋生活简单的原始社会，认为物质的丰富反而毁坏了人们的淳朴，渴望出现"小国寡民"的理想社会。"小国寡民"的意思就国家很小、国民稀少。在这样的理想社会里，人们不用辛劳、不用冒险、不用迁徙、不用打仗；人们恢复古代"结绳记事"的生活方法，吃得香甜，穿得舒服，住得安适，遵守原有的风俗习惯，在自己的岗位上快乐地工作。人人专心做自己的事情，各司其职，各守本分，一辈子也不往来。

老子的社会理想在当时有鲜明的针对性和批判性，但也有明显的局限性，人类社会必定要依靠相互合作才能得到不断发展。

Live in Peace and Work Happily

❖ **Paraphrase**

Live in peace and work happily.

❖ **Source**

Laozi: The people are willing to live on their own food, dress well, settle down to their own customs, and enjoy their own work, not visiting each other all their lives.

Laozi or Lao Tzu, a native of Chu State during the Spring and Autumn Period is an ancient Chinese thinker, philosopher, writer, and founder of the Taoist school, whose representative work is *Tao Te Ching*.

Laozi's last name is Li and given name is Er. There is a legend about the origin of Laozi's name. It was said that when Laozi was born, he was already full of grey hair, like a little old man with a white beard, so he was called "Laozi" ("Lao" means "old", and "zi" means "an **intellectual**" in Chinese). Laozi could talk as soon as he was born. He pointed to a plum ("Li" in Chinese) tree in the yard and said, "Li is my surname." And because his ears were so big, his given name was "Er" ("ear").

Laozi lived in the Spring and Autumn and Warring States period, with complicated social **contradictions**, constant wars, and extremely unstable life. Laozi admired

intellectual

n. 智者

contradiciton

n. 矛盾，对立

the primitive society with simple life very much. He believed that material **abundance** destroyed people's simplicity and longed for an ideal society of "small country with few people", which means that the country is small and the people are **scarce**. In such an ideal society there would be no toil, no risk, no migration, and no war; people restore the ancient way of life of "keep records by tying knots", eating tasty food, wearing and living comfortably, abiding by the original customs and habits, and working happily at their posts. Everyone concentrates on their own business, performs their own duties, and never interacts for a lifetime.

Laozi's social ideal was quite targeted and critical at that time, but it also had obvious limitations in that human society must rely on **cooperation** to achieve continuous development.

abundance
n. 丰盛，充裕

scarce
adj. 稀少的

cooperation
n. 合作

按图索骥

【释义】 按照画像去寻找好马。比喻办事死板，不懂得变通。
【出处】《汉书·梅福传》："犹察伯乐之图，求骐骥于市，而不可得。"

春秋时期，秦国有个名叫孙阳的人，善于鉴别马的好坏，人称"伯乐"——传说伯乐是负责管理天上马匹的神。孙阳把自己多年积累的经验写成一本书，名为《相马经》，图文并茂地介绍了各类好马。

孙阳的儿子很想继承父亲的事业，他把父亲的书背得滚瓜烂熟，就对父亲说，他已经学到了父亲的所有本领。父亲说："那你找一匹千里马来给我看看。"儿子满口答应，带着《相马经》就出发了。

《相马经》上说："千里马的主要特征是：额头隆起，双眼突出，四蹄犹如垒起的酒药饼子。"他按照这个特征找了很久，也没有什么收获。直到有一天，他发现路边有一只蹦蹦跳跳的动物，看了很久，越看越像，于是费了九牛二虎之力，才把这"千里马"捉住，带回家向父亲汇报。

一进门，他就嚷着说："我找到了一匹千里马，它长得和书中说的差不多，就是个头小了点，蹄子差了些。"

孙阳一看儿子送来的居然是一只癞蛤蟆，真是哭笑不得："傻儿子，你找到的是一只癞蛤蟆，根本不是什么千里马啊！你这样按图索骥是不行的，要学相马的本领，就得多去看马、养马，深入地了解马才行啊！"

儿子听了羞愧不已，从此便一头钻到马群中去研究马。

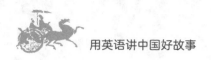

Look for a Steed with Its Picture

Paraphrase

Look for a steed only according to its picture. This idiom describes people who are **inflexible**, trying to find something by following a single clue.

inflexible
adj. 死板的，顽固的

Source

Biography of Mei Fu, Book of Han: Although having closely observed the picture of a steed in the book written by Bo Le, you can't find it in the market.

During the Spring and Autumn Period, there was a man named Sun Yang in Qin State who was good at distinguishing the quality of horses. He was called Bo Le. Legend has it that Bo Le was the god responsible for managing the horses in the heaven. Sun Yang wrote a book about his years of experience, called *Xiang Ma Jing* (the Art of Judging Horses), which introduces all kinds of good horses in both pictures and texts.

Sun Yang's son wanted to carry on his father's business. He memorized his father's book thoroughly and told his father that he had learned all his father's skills. His father said, "Then you find a winged steed to show me." The son readily promised, and set off with *Xiang Ma Jing*.

The book wrote, "The main features of a winged steed

are a raised forehead, **protruding** eyes, and four hoofs like piled-up Chinese yeast cakes." He searched for a long time, but nothing was gained. Until one day, he found a bouncing animal on the roadside. After watching it for a long time, he found it fit the features, so he tried very hard to catch this "winged steed" and took it home to his father.

As soon as he entered the door, he yelled, "I found a winged steed. It looks almost the same as the book says, but it's a bit smaller and has slightly worse hooves."

When Sun Yang saw that his son had sent a **toad**, he was really dumbfounded, "Silly son, what you found is a toad, not a winged steed at all! It's impossible to find a steed only with its picture. If you want to learn the skills of judging horses, you must observe them, raise them, and learn more about them!"

Hearing this, the son was so ashamed that he kept himself into the barn to study them thereafter.

protruding
adj. 突出的

toad
n. 癞蛤蟆

百步穿杨

【释义】在一百步远以外射中杨柳的叶子。形容箭法十分高明。

【出处】《史记·周本纪》:"楚有养由基者,善射;去柳叶百步而射之,百发百中。"

春秋时,楚国有一位著名射手,叫养由基,年轻时就勇力过人,练成了一手好箭法。当时还有一个射手,叫潘虎,也是箭术过人。他们互相看不起对方,都以为自己的箭术天下第一。

他们约好来一场公开赛,引来很多人围观。靶子设在五十步外,那里竖起一块板,板上有一个红心。潘虎拉开射箭,一连三箭都正中红心,博得一片喝彩声。潘虎洋洋得意地向养由基拱手说:"请多多指教!"语气里带有明显挑衅,仿佛在说,就看你能不能射得比我更准。

没想到,养由基只是不屑一顾地笑笑,说:"射中五十步外的红心,算什么本领?目标太近、太大了,不如射百步外的柳叶吧!"

潘虎听说他要射一百步外的柳叶,觉得他是在说大话,根本做不到,嘴上不说什么,心想着看养由基的笑话。

养由基指着百步外的一棵杨柳树,叫人在树上选一片叶子,涂上红色作为靶子。接着,他拉开弓,"嗖"的一声,射出的箭正好贯穿了这片杨柳叶的中心。在场所有人都被眼前的情形惊呆了。

潘虎也暗暗惊奇,世上竟然有这么高明的箭术,他自叹不如,又不甘心,心想对方不可能箭箭都那么准,没有失误。于是他便走到那棵杨柳树下,选择了三片柳树叶子,在上面用不同的颜色编号,请养由基按编号次序再射,一边幸灾乐祸地等着养由基出丑。

养由基向前走几步,看清了编号,然后退到百步之外,拉弓瞄准,"嗖""嗖""嗖",三箭连发,分别射中三片编上号的杨柳叶。潘虎情不自禁地大声惊呼:"好箭法!"人群中也发出一片喝彩声。

Shoot Willow Leaves a Hundred Steps away

Paraphrase

Shoot a willow leaf a hundred steps away. It is used to describe excellent skills in archery.

Source

Basic Annals of Zhou, Records of the Grand Historian: there was a man called Yang Youji in Chu State, who was good at shooting. He shot willow leaves a hundred steps away with great accuracy.

In the Spring and Autumn Period, there lived a famous archer named Yang Youji in Chu State, who had great courage when he was young and became a good archer. There was also an archer called Pan Hu, who was also excellent at shooting. They looked down on each other, both thinking that their shooting skills were the best in the world.

They made an appointment for a public match, which attracted many onlookers. The target was set fifty steps away, and a board was **erected** there with a red heart on it. Pan Hu pulled away and shot his arrows. Three arrows hit the red heart, winning a lot of cheers. Pan Hu **triumphantly** said to Yang Youji, "Please give me some advice!" That seemed to be an obvious **provocation**, as if to say, "How can you shoot better than me?"

erect
v. 竖立，搭起
triumphantly
adv. 得意洋洋地
provocation
n. 挑衅

Unexpectedly, Yang Youji just smiled **dismissively**, and said, "What is the meaning to shoot a red heart fifty steps away? The target is too close and too big. Why not shoot a willow leaf a hundred steps away!"

Pan Hu heard that Yang Youji was going to shoot willow leaves a hundred paces away, and felt that Yang Youji was **bragging** and couldn't do it at all. He didn't say anything, but thought about watching Yang Youji become a laughing stock.

Yang Youji pointed to a willow tree a hundred steps away and asked someone to choose a leaf on the tree and paint it red as a target. Then, he drew his bow, with a "**whoosh**", and the arrow just pierced through the center of the willow leaf. Everyone present was **stunned** by what they saw.

Pan Hu was also surprised that there was such brilliant shooting skills in the world. He sighed that his skills was not as good as Yang Youji's, but he was not willing to admit it. So he walked under the willow tree, chose three willow leaves, and numbered them in different colors. He asked Yang Yuji to shoot again in the order of the numbers, while waiting for him to make a fool of himself.

Yang Youji walked a few steps forward and saw the numbers clearly, then stepped back a hundred steps away. He drew his bow, aimed at the targets, "whoosh" "whoosh" and "whoosh", shot three arrows in a row, and hit three numbered willow leaves respectively. Pan Hu couldn't help but **exclaimed**, "Excellent shooting skills!" The crowd also burst into cheers.

---

dismissively
adv. 轻蔑地

brag
v. 吹嘘

whoosh
n. 嗖的一声，呼的一声

stun
v. 使震惊

exclaim
v. 惊呼，呼喊

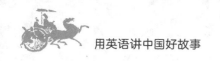

杯弓蛇影

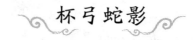

【释义】误把映入酒杯中的弓影当作蛇。比喻疑神疑鬼,自相惊扰。

【出处】《风俗通义·怪神》:"时北壁上有悬赤弩照于杯中,其形如蛇。"

晋朝有一个叫乐广的人,喜欢结交朋友,经常请朋友到家里喝酒聊天。这一天,乐广又和朋友们饮酒作乐,有位朋友饮酒后突然悄悄走了,乐广心里纳闷,很想知道什么原因。此后一直没有见到这位朋友,乐广放心不下,于是亲自登门拜访,才知道这位朋友已经生病好几天了,仍然不见好转。乐广非常好奇,问他那天喝酒时还好好的,怎么一下子病得这么厉害。

朋友支支吾吾,欲说又止。在乐广一再追问下,朋友才说出实情。原来那天喝酒时,朋友突然发现自己的酒杯里有一条蛇,还在慢慢地蠕动,当时就恶心极了,但想到主人敬酒,盛情难却,大家都非常开心,不能扫了大家的兴,就强忍着喝了那杯酒,然后不辞而别。回家后感到全身难受,总感觉自己肚子里有一条小蛇,怀疑自己中毒了,于是一病不起。

得知朋友的情况,乐广也是一头雾水,他回到家中仔细察看,突然发现墙上挂着一张弯弓,顿时恍然大悟。乐广再次把朋友请到家中,模仿聚会时举杯敬酒的情形,朋友刚举起杯子,突然又看到杯中有小蛇在游动,非常惊恐。乐广连忙指着墙上挂着的弓,对朋友说:"都是它在作怪,杯中的小蛇就是这张弓的影子!"乐广又把弓从墙上取下,这时朋友杯中的小蛇也消失了。这位朋友知道真相后,不再疑神疑鬼,很快病就好了。

Mistake the Shadow of a Bow in the Cup as a Snake

❖ **Paraphrase**

Mistake the shadow of a bow reflected in the cup as a snake. It is a metaphor for being jittery with imaginary fear.

❖ **Source**

Guaishen, Fengsu Tongyi: At that time, there was a big red bow hung on the north wall of the house, and the shadow of the bow just shining in the wine cup, shaped like a snake.

There was a man called Le Guang in the Jin Dynasty who liked to make friends and often invited them to drink and chat at home. One day, Le Guang was drinking and having fun with his friends again. A friend suddenly went away quietly after drinking. Le Guang was puzzled and wanted to know the reason. Since then, he had not seen his friend for a long time. Le Guang felt uneasy and went to visit him in person. Only then did he know that the friend had been ill for several days and was still not getting better. Le Guang was very curious and asked him why he had been so ill after he drank that day.

His friend hesitated and stopped talking. After Le

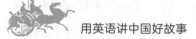

Guang asked repeatedly, his friend told the truth. It turned out that when he was drinking that day, his friend suddenly noticed that there was a snake in his cup, which was still **squirming** slowly. It was very **disgusting**. But thinking of the **hospitality** of the host, and everyone being very happy, he didn't want to discourage others. He unwillingly drank the wine, and then left without saying goodbye. After returning home, he felt uncomfortable all over, and felt that there was a small snake in his stomach. He suspected that he had been poisoned and fell ill since then.

Le Guang was at a loss when he learned about his friend's situation. He returned home to take a closer look, and suddenly found a bow hanging on the wall, then realized what had happened. Le Guang invited his friend to the house again and imitated the situation of toasting at the party. The friend just raised the cup and again saw a small snake swimming in the cup. He was very frightened. Le Guang quickly pointed to the bow hanging on the wall, and said to his friend, "It is the bow that is causing the trouble. The snake in the cup is the shadow of the bow!" Le Guang took the bow off the wall and the snake in the cup disappeared. After the friend knew the truth, he stopped being **suspicious**, and soon recovered from the illness.

squirm

v. 蠕动

disgusting

adj. 恶心的

hospitality

n. 好客

suspicious

adj. 怀疑的, 不信任的

鞭长莫及

【释义】 虽然鞭子长,但也打不到马肚子上。后来借指力量达不到。

【出处】《左传·宣公十五年》:"虽鞭之长,不及马腹。"

春秋时期,楚庄王派申舟访问齐国,途中必经宋国。按照常理,经过宋国应事先通知宋国,然而楚庄王自恃楚国为大国,不把宋国放在眼里,就没有通知宋国。宋国国君知道后,十分气愤,将申舟扣留下来。大臣华元对国君说:"楚国事先没有通知我国,就是眼中没有我们宋国,把我国当作已经灭亡了,领土也都归属于楚国,这真是欺人太甚。我们必须维护独立主权的尊严,不受这种侮辱!杀了申舟,警告楚王,即使引发楚国的入侵战争,也在所不惜,大不了就是亡国,宋国也不服屈辱!"

宋国国君听了大臣华元的话,处死了申舟,并做好随时抵抗楚国入侵的准备。楚庄王得知申舟被杀,果然发兵攻打宋国,并将宋国都城团团围住。但宋国上下一心,坚决抵抗,相持了好几个月,楚国也没能取胜。

宋国毕竟是个小国,哪里经得起长时间的战争消耗。第二年春,宋国派人向晋国求助。晋景公正准备出兵相助,有大臣劝阻说:"'虽鞭长,不及马腹(鞭子再长,也打不到马的肚子)',我们又怎能管得了楚国呢?宋国来人求救,我们如果不答应,确实不合情理,心中感到有些耻辱,但如今楚国强大,我们不能得罪楚国,为晋国考虑,您还是忍一忍吧。"

景公听了大臣的话,停止发兵救宋,改派使者专程回访宋国,叫宋国不要投降,并有意放话,说援兵已经出发,很快就到。宋国人得到鼓舞,看到希望,战斗力得到爆发,又坚持了几个月,楚军久攻不下,最后与宋国议和,只得带走宋国大臣华元作为人质,战争终告结束。

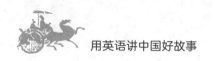

Even a Long Whip Can't Reach It

Paraphrase

Although the whip is very long, it could not hit the horse's belly. Later it means a person is not capable of doing something.

Source

The Fifteenth Year of Duke Xuan of Lu, Zuo Zhuan: "Long as the whip is, it can not reach the horse's belly."

During the Spring and Autumn Period, King Zhuang of Chu sent Shen Zhou to visit Qi State, and he must pass through Song State on the way. According to common practice, Song State should be informed in advance. However, King Zhuang of Chu thought that Chu State was a big state, so he did not notify Song State. When the King of Song learned this, he was very angry and detained Shen Zhou. Hua Yuan, one of the ministers, said to the King, "Chu State has not informed us in advance. THe people there look down upon our state. They treat us as if our state has been destroyed and that all the **territory** belongs to them. They've gone too far in **insulting** us! We must uphold the **sovereignty** and fight back! Kill Shen Zhou to warn King Zhuang of Chu. Even if it will lead to an invasion of Chu State, we should do so at all costs. At worst, we will be conquered. We shall not submit to the

territory
n. 领土
insult
v. 侮辱
sovereignty
n. 主权

humiliation!"

King of Song listened to his minister Hua Yuan. He put Shen Zhou to death, and made preparations to resist the invasion of Chu State at any time. When King Zhuang of Chu learned that Shen Zhou had been killed, he sent troops to attack Song State and **surrounded** its capital. However, the people of Song State united and resolutely resisted for several months, and Chu State failed to win the battle.

Song State, after all, as a small country, could not **withstand** a long war. In the spring of the following year, Song State sent a messenger to Jin State for help. When Duke Jing of Jin was about to send the army to help Song State, a minister **dissuaded** him, saying, "Though the whip is long, it can't reach a horse's belly. How can we control Chu State over this matter? It would be unreasonable and a little bit ashamed if we did not help Song State. But now Chu State is strong and we cannot offend it. For the sake of Jin, you had better think it over."

Duke Jing listened to his minister. He stopped sending troops to save Song State, while sent messengers to pay a special visit to Song State. He asked Song State not to surrender, and revealed that **reinforcements** had already set off and would soon arrive. The people of Song State were encouraged and saw hope. Their fighting ability burst out and they held out for several more months. For a long time, the army of Chu State could not defeat Song State. Finally, they made peace with Song State and took away their minister Hua Yuan as a **hostage**. The war ended.

humiliation

n. 屈辱

surround

v. 围绕，环绕

withstand

v. 忍受

dissuade

v. 劝阻

reinforcement

n. 援军

hostage

n. 人质

不为五斗米折腰

【释义】比喻为人不庸俗,有骨气,不为利禄所动。
【出处】《晋书·陶潜传》:"吾不能为五斗米折腰,拳拳事乡里小人邪。"

　　陶渊明是东晋后期的大诗人、文学家,出生于官宦家庭,曾祖父陶侃是东晋开国功臣,祖父和父亲都曾在朝为官。

　　东晋末期,朝政日益腐败,官场黑暗。陶渊明生性淡泊名利,为官清正,不愿与腐败官员同流合污,辞职过起了隐居生活。陶渊明最后一次做官,是公元405年秋,那时他刚过"不惑之年"(41岁),在朋友的劝说下,到离家不远的彭泽出任县令。到任第81天,上级派督察来彭泽巡查。这个督察非常傲慢无礼,一到彭泽就住进宾馆休息,派人喊县令来拜见他。陶渊明本来正要去拜见督察,正好看到县吏匆忙跑来传达督察要他去宾馆拜见的口令,县吏见陶渊明身着便装前往,连忙提醒道:"大人参见督察,应该着官服前往,以免督察心生不快,与大人过不去,对大人不利。"

　　陶渊明平时就蔑视功名富贵,不肯趋炎附势,对这种假借上司名义发号施令的人更是瞧不起。当时县令只有五斗米的官俸,陶渊明叹息道:"我不能为五斗米折腰,向那些小人献殷勤。"说完,就将县令的官印交还,从此弃职而去,归隐田园,成为中国第一位田园诗人。

Won't Bow for Five *Dou* of Rice

❧ Paraphrase

This is a metaphor to describe people with elegance and integrity, who will not bow to wealth and power.

❧ Source

The Biography of Tao Qian, Book of Jin: I can't bend my waist to this village **villain** because of five *dou* of rice.

villain

n. 恶棍，坏人

Tao Yuanming was a great poet and writer in the late Eastern Jin Dynasty. He was born in an official family, whose great-grandfather Tao Kan was the founding hero of the Eastern Jin Dynasty. Both his grandfather and father were officials.

In the late Eastern Jin Dynasty, the government became increasingly corrupt. Tao Yuanming was honest and upright in office, caring little about fame and wealth. He was unwilling to associate himself with corrupt officials, so he resigned and lived a reclusive life. The last time Tao Yuanming became an official was in the autumn of 405 AD. At that time, he had just passed "The Age of No-doubt" (41 years old). Under the persuasion of his friends, he went to Pengze, not far from his home, as the county **magistrate**. On the 81st day of his appointment, the superior sent an inspector to Pengze for inspection.

magistrate

n. 地方执法官

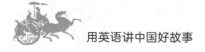

This inspector was very arrogant and rude, and as soon as he arrived in Pengze, he went to a hotel to rest and sent someone to call the county magistrate to visit him. Tao Yuanming was about to go to see the inspector when he saw the county official rushing to deliver the message that the inspector asked him to go to the hotel. The county official saw Tao dressed in casual clothes and immediately reminded him, "My lord, you should wear official clothes to see the inspector, so as not to upset the inspector and get in trouble with him."

Tao Yuanming always **despised** fame and wealth, and refused to please those in power. He especially looked down upon those who gave orders under the guise of their superiors. At that time, the county magistrate only had a salary of five brackets of rice. Tao Yuanming sighed, "I can't bow for five brackets of rice and show courtesy to those villains." With that, he returned the seal of the county magistrate, abandoned his post and went to live in the countryside, and then became the first pastoral poet in China.

despise

v. 蔑视

成语故事

草木皆兵

【释义】把山上的草木都当作敌兵。形容人在惊慌时疑神疑鬼。
【出处】《晋书·苻坚载记》:"北望八公山上草森皆类人形。"

公元 4 世纪,南北朝时期,以黄河为界,古代中国形成了南北对峙的局面。前秦皇帝苻坚统一了北方黄河流域,想以秋风扫落叶之势,一举消灭偏安江南的东晋,统一天下。

公元 383 年 5 月,苻坚率领八十多万军队开始进攻东晋,很快攻下了寿阳。寿阳就是今天的安徽寿县,离东晋首都金陵——今天的南京已经不远了。

大兵压境,东晋军队只有八万人,不到苻坚大军的十分之一。苻坚派人去劝降东晋军队,没想到派的使者原来就是东晋的官员,对东晋仍然有着深厚的感情,不仅没有劝降,反而把秦军的部署和弱点,一五一十地告诉了晋军,并建议晋军偷袭秦军在洛涧(今安徽省淮南市)的先头部队。晋军听计,突袭洛涧,秦军仓促应战,很快溃不成军,晋军乘胜追击,一直追到淝水(今淝河,在安徽省寿县)东岸,抢占八公山高地,与驻扎寿阳的秦军隔岸对峙。

苻坚得知洛涧兵败,大惊失色,马上登上寿阳城头,亲自观察淝水对岸的晋军动静。时值隆冬,阴云密布,远远望去,淝水上空灰蒙蒙一片,只见对岸晋军一座座营帐排列得整整齐齐,手持刀枪的晋兵来往巡逻,阵容严整威武。再往远处看,对面八公山上,隐隐约约不知道有多少晋兵。其实,八公山上并没有晋兵,不过是苻坚心虚眼花,把八公山上的草木都看作是晋兵了。随着一阵西北风呼啸而过,山上晃动的草木,就像无数士兵在走动。苻坚顿时面如土色,惊恐不已。

不久,晋军渡过淝水,与秦军决一死战,苻坚被箭射伤,只带了十多万人逃回长安。这就是历史上有名的以少胜多的"淝水之战"。

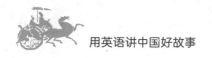

Every Bushes and Trees Look like Enemies

Paraphrase

Treat the bushes and trees on the mountain as enemies. This idiom refers to people who are suspicious when they are in panic.

Source

The Biography of Fu Jian, Book of Jin: To the north, the trees and grass on Bagong Mountain all looked like soldiers.

In the 4th century, during the Northern and Southern Dynasties, with the Yellow River as the boundary, ancient China formed a **confrontation** between the North and the South. In the north, the Emperor of Former Qin State, Fu Jian, unified the Yellow River Basin, and wanted to wipe out the Eastern Jin Dynasty in the south of the Yangtze River with one blow to unify the country.

confrontation

n. 对抗，对峙

In May 383, Fu Jian led more than 800,000 troops to attack the Eastern Jin Dynasty and soon captured Shouyang. Shouyang is today's Shou County in Anhui province, not far from Jinling, the capital of the Eastern Jin Dynasty—today's Nanjing.

With soldiers pressing down on the border, the Eastern Jin army had only 80,000 soldiers, less than a

成语故事

tenth of Fu Jian's army. Fu Jian sent an **envoy** to persuade the Eastern Jin army to surrender, but it turned out that the envoy was a former official of the Eastern Jin Dynasty and had a deep affection for it. Instead of persuading Jin army to surrender, he told them the deploy and weaknesses of Qin army in full detail, and suggested Jin army plan a surprise attack on Qin army's front troops at Luojian (now Huainan, Anhui Province). Jin army followed the plan and attacked Luojian. Qin army was in a rush and was soon defeated. Jin army pursued its victory and reached the east bank of Feishui (now Fei River in Shou County, Anhui province). Jin army seized the height of Bagong Mountain, and faced off against Qin army stationed in Shouyang across the bank.

envoy

n. 使者，使节

When Fu Jian learned that Luojian was conquered, he was shocked, and immediately boarded the top of Shouyang City to observe the movement of the Jin army on the other side of Fei River. It was midwinter and the clouds were overcast. From a distance, the sky over the Fei River was gray. It could be seen that Jin army's camps on the opposite side lined up neatly and its soldiers were **patrolling** with swords and spears. Jin army was in perfect order. Looking further away, on the opposite side of Bagong Mountain, one could not exactly tell how many soldiers of Jin there were. In fact, there were no soldiers of Jin on Bagong Mountain, but Fu Jian was frightened and dazzled, so he regarded the bushes and trees on Bagong Mountain as soldiers of Jin. With a gust of northwest wind,

partrol

v. 巡逻，巡查

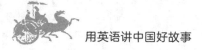

the **swaying** bushes and trees on the mountain looked like countless soldiers in motion, and Fu Jian's face turned pale with fright at once.

sway

v. 摇摆

Soon, Jin army crossed Feishui and fought to the death with the Qin army. Fu Jian was wounded by an arrow and fled back to Chang'an with only over 100,000 soldiers. This is the famous "Battle of Fei River" in history, in which the few defeated the many.

程门立雪

【释义】 本指学生恭敬受教，现指求学心切和尊师重教。

【出处】《宋史·杨时传》："颐既觉，则门外雪深一尺矣。"

程颢和程颐是两兄弟，同时受业于宋代著名理学大师周敦颐。他们两人学业有成，名气很大，被当时的人们尊称为"二程"，拜他们为师求学的人很多。

宋代学者杨时和游酢，先拜程颢为师。程颢去世后，他们虽然都已40多岁了，也都考上了进士，但仍然想进一步深造，就一起去拜程颐为师。

杨时和游酢登门拜访那天，在窗外看见程颐正在屋里闭目养神，就悄悄站在门外边等候，不忍心打扰老师。这时下起了大雪，而且越下越大，杨时和游酢仍然恭恭敬敬地站在雪地里，等候老师醒来。当程颐醒来发现他们时，门外的积雪已经有一尺多深了。

程颐被他俩真心求学和尊敬老师的行为深深打动，答应了他们拜师求学的请求。

The Snow Piles up at Cheng Yi's Door

❧ Paraphrase

Originally it refers to students who are respectful in their education, but now it is used to describe students who are eager to learn and respect their teachers.

❧ Source

The Biography of Yang Shi, History of Song: By the time Cheng Yi noticed, the snow outside the door was already more than a foot deep.

Cheng Hao and Cheng Yi were brothers who were both educated by Zhou Dunyi, a famous Neo-Confucianist in the Song Dynasty. They were very successful in their studies and very famous. They were respected as "Two Cheng" by the people at the time, and many people **worshiped** them as teachers and wanted to learn from them.

The scholars Yang Shi and You Zuo of the Song Dynasty at first were students of Cheng Hao. After Cheng Hao passed away, although both of them were in their 40s and were admitted to "jinshi"(a successful candidate in the highest imperial examinations), they still wanted to further their studies, so they went to visit Cheng Yi to be his students.

worship
v. 崇拜，敬仰

On the day when Yang Shi and You Zuo paid the visit, they saw Cheng Yi closing his eyes for rest from outside the window, so they quietly stood by the door and waited, and couldn't bear to disturb the teacher. It was snowing heavily at this time, and getting heavier and heavier. Yang Shi and You Zuo were still standing respectfully in the snow, waiting for the teacher to wake up. When Cheng Yi woke up and found them, the snow outside was more than a foot deep.

Cheng Yi was deeply moved by their sincere desire to study and their respect for teachers, and agreed to be their teacher.

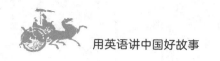

寸阴尺璧

【释义】阴：日影，光阴。寸阴：指极短的时间。日影移动一寸的时间价值比径尺的璧玉还要珍贵。形容时间可贵。

【出处】《淮南子·原道训》："故圣人不贵尺之璧而重寸之阴，时难得而易失也。"

禹是中国古代与尧、舜齐名的贤圣帝王，他最卓著的功绩，就是历来被传颂的治理滔天洪水，又划定中国版图为九州。后人称他为大禹。

民间流传着大禹珍惜时间的故事，如"禹不拾履"。夏禹为了不失去宝贵的时间，走路时鞋子掉了，却没有功夫去拾；帽子被风吹落在树枝上，也顾不上看一眼。他不是争着走在前面，而是珍惜大好时光为民造福。所以，明智的人，不认为尺璧是宝贵的，而重视寸阴的价值，因为时光难得却容易失去，一寸光阴一寸金，寸金难买寸光阴。

Time Is More Precious than Jade

❧ Paraphrase

The time it takes the sun's shadow to move by an inch is more valuable than the jade one foot long, which means time is very precious.

❧ Source

Searching out Tao, Huainanzi: Therefore, the sages value an inch of time more than an inch of jade, in that time is hard to gain while easy to lose.

Yu was a sage emperor of ancient China on a par with Yao and Shun. His most outstanding achievement was to control the floods and delimit the territory of China as Jiuzhou or Nine Provinces. Later generations called him Great Yu.

There is a story of Yu's cherishing time, which is called "Yu didn't pick up his shoes". Yu lost his shoes while walking, but he did not have the time to pick them up in order to save precious time; his hat was blown by the wind and fell on the branch, but he didn't cast a glance at it. He was not striving to be ahead, but cherishing the time to benefit the people. Therefore, a wise man does not think that a foot length of jade is as valuable as a moment of time, because time is rare and easy to lose. An inch of gold is hard to exchange an inch of time.

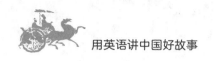

道旁苦李

【释义】路边的苦李,走过的人不摘取。比喻不被重视的人或事。

【出处】《晋书·王戎传》:"树在道边而多子,必苦李也。"

王戎,魏晋时期名士,是"竹林七贤"中年龄最小的一位。王戎出身于官宦家庭,自幼聪明好学。7岁那年,有一次他和几个小伙伴一块儿外出游玩。大家玩累了口渴,都在找水喝,这时有个孩子发现路边有几株李树,树上还有不少李子,看上去一个个都熟透了,就招呼大家去摘李子解渴。小伙伴们一个个高兴地爬到树上,争先恐后地摘李子,只有王戎一个人站在原地,对小伙伴们喊道:"别摘了,那些李子是苦的,不能吃!"

没有人相信他的话。小伙伴们兴高采烈地带着李子下树了,他们刚咬一口,一个个都龇牙咧嘴,"呸呸"吐不停,一边吐一边嚷道:"太苦了!"

伙伴们好奇起来,问王戎怎么知道树上的李子是苦的。王戎笑着说:"你看,这李树都长在路边,上面结了那么多李子,却没有人摘,要不是苦的,能会这样吗?"

大家都非常佩服王戎。王戎长大做官后,仍然保持这种经常观察、推理和思考的习惯,为国家选拔了大量优秀人才。

成语故事

Bitter Plums by the Roadside

Paraphrase

The bitter plums by the roadside are not picked by passersby. This is a metaphor for people or things that are not taken seriously.

Source

The Biography of Wang Rong, Book of Jin: If plum trees are growing by the roadside with many plums, the plums are sure to be bitter ones.

Wang Rong, a celebrity during the Wei and Jin Dynasties, was the youngest among the "Seven **Sages** of the Bamboo Grove". Born into an official family, Wang Rong was clever and eager to learn since his childhood. When he was 7 years old, he once went out to play with a few friends. Everyone was tired and thirsty. They wondered where they could find water. At this time, one of them noticed that there were a few plum trees by the roadside, and there were many plums on the trees, all of which seemed ripe, so he asked the friends to pick the plums. Everyone, except Wang Rong, climbed up to the tree happily and rushed to pick the plums. Only Wang Rong stood alone and shouted to his friends, "Don't pick them. Those plums are bitter and you can't eat them!"

sage

n. 圣人，智者

No one believed him. His friends happily took the plums down the tree. As soon as they had taken a bite, they all looked painful and spat it all out, exclaiming as they did so, "How bitter!"

The friends became curious and asked Wang Rong how he knew the plums were bitter. Wang Rong said with a smile, "Well, these plum trees are growing by the roadside with so many plums on them, but no one picks them. If it were not bitter, would it be like this?"

Everyone admired Wang Rong very much. After Wang Rong grew up and became an official, he still maintained this habit of observation, **reasoning** and thinking, and selected a large number of excellent talents for the country.

reason
v. 推理，推断

道听途说

【释义】 路上听来的、路上传播的话。指没有根据的传闻。
【出处】《论语·阳货》:"道听而途说,德之弃也。"

战国时期,齐国有个人叫毛空,喜欢把听来的没有根据的事情,再津津有味地讲给别人听。有一天,艾子带着学生从楚国回到齐国,刚进都城,就遇到了爱说空话的毛空。毛空极其神秘地告诉艾子,有个人家有一只神奇的鸭子,一次生下一百个蛋。

艾子不信,说:"哪有这样奇怪的事情!"

毛空说:"那可能是两只鸭子下的蛋。"

艾子摇摇头:"这也不可能。"

毛空连忙改口说:"那大概是三只鸭子下的吧。"

艾子还是不信。

"那也可能是四只、八只、十只。"艾子当然不相信他的话。

见艾子不信,毛空又想了想,对艾子说:"上个月,天上掉下一块肉来,有三十丈长、十丈宽。"

艾子不信,毛空急忙改口说:"那么是二十丈长。"

艾子还是不信。

毛空说:"那就算十丈吧!"

艾子实在忍不住了,再也不愿意听毛空瞎说了,反问道:"你亲眼看见从天上掉下来肉吗?你亲眼见过那只下蛋的鸭子吗?"

毛空答不出话来,支支吾吾地说:"那都是我在路上听人家说的。"

艾子听后,笑了,转身对站在身后的学生们说:"你们可不要像他那样'道

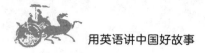

听途说'啊!"

孔子曾经说过:"从路上听来的没有根据的话,再不负责任地传播,这种捕风捉影的做法,为有道德的人所唾弃。"

Hear and Spread on the Road

Paraphrase

Words heard and spread on the road. This idiom refers to groundless rumors.

Source

Yanghuo, *The Analects*: He who hears words on the road and then spread it will be rejected by moral people.

During the Warring States Period, there was a man called Mao Kong in Qi State. He liked to tell others vividly about things that were **groundless**. One day, Aizi and his students returned from Chu State to Qi State. As soon as they entered the capital, they met Mao Kong, who was fond of empty talk. Mao Kong told Aizi very mysteriously that there was a man who had a magic duck, which laid 100 eggs at a time.

Aizi didn't believe it, and said, "How can there be such a strange thing!"

Mao Kong said, "That might be the eggs laid by two ducks."

Aizi shook his head, "It's impossible."

Mao Kong quickly changed his words and said, "Then it's probably three ducks."

Aizi still didn't believe it.

groundless *adj.* 无根据的，无理的

"That could be four, eight, or ten." Aizi certainly didn't believe his words.

Seeing Aizi's distrust, Mao Kong thought about it again, and said to Aizi, "Last month, a piece of meat fell from the sky. It is 100-meter long and 30-meter wide."

Aizi didn't believe it. Mao Kong hurriedly changed his words and said, "Then it is 60-meter long."

Aizi still didn't believe it.

Mao Kong said, "Then it must be 30-meter long!"

Aizi couldn't bear it anymore, and no longer wanted to listen to Mao Kong's nonsense, and asked, "Did you see the meat falling from the sky or the duck laying eggs with your own eyes?"

Mao Kong couldn't answer, and he said, "That's all I heard from others on the road."

After hearing this, Aizi laughed, turned around and said to the students standing behind him, "Don't learn from him!"

Confucius once said, "If you hear groundless words from the road, and then spread them **irresponsibly**, this kind of behavior will be rejected by people with morals."

irresponsibly
adv. 不负责任地

东施效颦

【释义】 比喻模仿别人，不但模仿不好，反而出丑，适得其反。

【出处】 《庄子·天运》："故西施病心而矉其里，其里之丑人见而美之，归亦捧心而矉其里。"

从前，越国有个出名的美女，叫西施。她的一举一动都让人感到很美。她因胸口痛，经常用双手捂着胸口，皱着眉头。但就是这种病态，也让她显得分外妩媚，楚楚动人。

同村有个长得很丑的女子，叫东施。她以为西施之所以美，就是因为经常捂着胸口、皱着眉头的样子。于是，东施也学着西施，一出门就用双手捂着胸口，把眉头皱得紧紧的，走一步扭一扭，装出一副弱不禁风的病态。东施的无病呻吟、矫揉造作，让人见了恶心。只要东施一出门，人们就赶紧把自家大门关上，不想看见。有的人连忙带着子女躲到远远的村外去，怕自己的孩子学坏了样子。

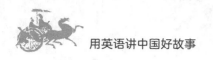

Dongshi Imitates the Beauty

◆ **Paraphrase**

This idiom refers to people who imitate someone they admire, but imitate badly, and make a fool of themselves.

◆ **Source**

Heavenly Revolutions, Zhuangzi: Xishi frowned and walked in the village because of chest pain. An ugly person in the village saw it and thought she was doing it beautifully. When returning home, the ugly person frowned and covered her chest, too.

Once upon a time, there was a famous beauty named Xishi in Yue State. Her every single move was attractive. She had a chest problem, so she often covered her chest with her hands and frowned. But even this posture made her look particularly charming.

There was a very ugly woman in the same village called Dongshi. She thought that the reason why Xishi was attractive was the way she often covered her chest and frowned. As a result, Dongshi followed suit. As soon as she went out, she covered her chest with her hands, **knit** her brows tightly, and walked with a twist, pretending to be weak. Dongshi's **affectation** made people feel sick. As soon as Dongshi went out, people quickly closed their

knit
v. 皱（眉）

affectation
n. 做作，装模作样

doors and didn't want to see her. Some people hurriedly took their children to hide outside of the village, fearing that their children would follow Dongshi's bad example.

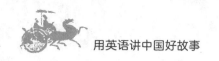

对牛弹琴

【释义】比喻对不讲道理的人讲道理，对不懂得美的人讲风雅。也用来讥讽人讲话时不看对象。

【出处】《理惑论》："公明仪为牛弹《清角》之操，伏食如故。非牛不闻，不合其耳也。"

战国时期，有个叫公明仪的人，精通音律，弹得一手好琴。

他对着一头老牛弹了一首名叫《清角》的名曲。公明仪自以为弹得十分精彩、动听，可那头老牛一点也不给面子，只是埋头吃草，像是没听见任何声音一样。其实并不是这头牛没有听见，只是乐曲不合它的耳朵。公明仪又用古琴模仿蚊子嗡嗡的叫声，还模仿离群的小牛发出的哀鸣声。那头老牛立刻停止了吃草，抬起头，竖起耳朵，摇着尾巴，东张西望起来，还不安地来回踏着小步，注意地听着。

Play the *Guqin* to a Cow

Paraphrase

The idiom is a metaphor which means to reason with unreasonable people, or talk about art with people who don't know how to appreciate it. It is also used to mock people who talk without considering the listeners.

Source

Lihuolun: Gong Mingyi played a piece of music called *Qingjiao* to a cow, but the old cow just buried his head in the grass. It's not that the cow didn't hear it, but that the music didn't please its ears.

During the Warring States Period, there was a man called Gong Mingyi who was good at playing the *guqin*.

One day, he played a famous piece of music called *Qingjiao* in front of an old cow. Gong Mingyi thought he was playing very well and beautifully, but the old cow didn't give any response, just buried his head in the grass, as if he hadn't heard any sound. It's not that the cow didn't hear it, but that the music didn't please its ears. Later Gong Mingyi played the *guqin* to imitate the buzzing of mosquitoes and the **wailing** of **stray** calves. The old cow stopped eating grass at once, raised his head, pricked up his ears, **wagged** his tail, looked around, and stepped restlessly to and fro, listening attentively.

wail

v. 哀号

stray

adj. 走失的，离群的

wag

v. 摇，摆动

多行不义必自毙

【释义】坏事干多了，必然会自取灭亡。
【出处】《左传·隐公元年》："多行不义必自毙，子姑待之。"

郑武公是春秋时期郑国第二任国君。他和夫人姜氏有两个儿子，大的叫庄生，小的叫共叔段。姜氏喜欢小儿子共叔段，经常在郑武公面前夸赞小儿子，想让郑武公传位给小儿子，郑武公一直没有答应。

郑武公死后，他的大儿子庄生继位，就是郑庄公。姜氏偏爱小儿子共叔段，要求郑庄公把制邑（今河南汜水县）封给共叔段，郑庄公没有答应。姜氏又要求郑庄公把京城（今河南荥阳）封给共叔段，因为这一要求也超过了当时的制度规定，郑庄公心里不愿意，但担心母亲姜氏因为自己的拒绝而非常生气，也不想引起兄弟不和，就勉强答应了。

没想到的是，共叔段到了京城后，倚仗着母亲的支持，私自招兵买马，囤积粮草，寻找机会，夺取哥哥的皇位。共叔段的行为已经路人皆知，大臣们纷纷觐见郑庄公，劝其早做准备，以防不测。郑庄公说："坏事做多了，必定会自取灭亡，你们就等着看吧！"

不久，共叔段的势力在不断扩大，趁郑庄公去洛阳朝见周天子的机会，和母亲姜氏里应外合，一举攻下郑都。原来郑庄公早有防备，不仅朝见周天子是个幌子，将郑都让给叛军也在计策之中，借此麻痹共叔段。事实上，郑庄公是避开叛军的锋芒，出奇兵攻取叛军的窝穴，受共叔段长久压迫的农民们，纷纷拥护郑庄公，参加讨伐叛军的战斗，郑庄公带着士气高昂的军队，打回郑都，共叔段兵败逃亡，被追兵逼到走投无路，自杀身亡。

Evil Deeds Bring about Self-destruction

Paraphrase

If you do too many bad things, you will certainly bring your own ruin.

Source

The First Year of Duke Yin, Zuo Zhuan: If you do too many bad things, you will surely ruin yourself. Just wait and see.

Duke Wu of Zheng was the second emperor of Zheng State in the Spring and Autumn Period. He and his wife Jiang had two sons. The oldest was called Zhuang Sheng, and the younger was called Gongshuduan. Jiang liked the younger son Gongshuduan, and often praised the younger son in front of Duke Wu, and wanted Duke Wu to pass the throne to the younger son, but Duke Wu did not agree.

After the death of Duke Wu, his eldest son, Zhuang Sheng, succeeded to the throne as Duke Zhuang of Zheng. Jiang liked her younger son Gongshuduan more, and asked Duke Zhuang to grant him Zhi city(now Sishui county, Henan). However, Duke Zhuang refused. Jiang asked Duke Zhuang to grant Gongshuduan Jing city(now Xingyang, Henan). This request also **violated** the **regulations** at that

violate
v. 违反，违背

regulation
n. 章程

分道扬镳

【释义】分道而行。也指因志趣、目标不同而各走各的路。

【出处】《魏书·河间公齐传》："洛阳我之丰沛，自应分路扬镳。自今以后，可分路而行。"

这是发生在南北朝北魏孝文帝时期的故事。当时北魏的首都在洛阳，担任地方官"洛阳令"的人叫元志，此人能言善辩，还有几分清高，对有权势的人，从不曲意奉承。

有一天，他和担任御史中尉的李彪在路上相遇，李彪的官位比他高，他却不避让，李彪很生气，当场训斥元志。元志不服，两人就争吵起来。

李彪说："我的官职比你高，你应该主动避让。"

元志也不示弱："我是洛阳令，在我管辖的范围里，我作为一地之主，怎么可以给住户让道？"

两人互不相让，决定一同觐见孝文帝，请孝文帝评理。

李彪说："我是御史中尉，职位比洛阳令高，他哪有资格与我抢道？"

元志说："我是洛阳地方官，普天之下有谁不用编户入籍？我怎么能像一个普通官员那样，去避让奉迎中尉呢？"

孝文帝听了，笑道："洛阳是我的都城，你们应该分道扬镳。从今以后，你们可以分开走，各走各的道吧！"

Go Separate Ways

Paraphrase

Go separate ways. It also refers to walking different paths due to different interests and goals.

Source

The Biography of Duke He Jian, Book of Wei: Luoyang is my capital, and you should split your way. From now on, you can go separately on your own way.

This story took place during the period of Emperor Xiaowen of the Northern Wei Dynasty. At that time, the capital of the Northern Wei State was Luoyang. The local official named Yuan Zhi was **eloquent** and somewhat lofty. He never flattered people with power and wealth.

One day, he met the censor Li Biao on the road. Li Biao's position was higher than Yuan Zhi, but Yuan Zhi did not give way to him. Li Biao was very angry, and **reprimanded** Yuan Zhi on the spot. Yuanzhi refused to accept the criticism, and quarreled with him.

Li Biao said, "I am the censor. My position is higher than yours. You should take the initiative to give way to me."

Yuan Zhi did not show weakness, "I am the magistrate

eloquent
adj. 雄辩的，有口才的

reprimand
v. 训斥

of Luoyang. As the landlord within my **jurisdiction**, how can I give way to the residents?"

The two refused to give in to each other, and decided to ask Emperor Xiaowen to judge who was right.

Li Biao said, "I am the censor, a higher position than the magistrate of Luoyang. How can he compete with me?"

Yuan Zhi said, "I am a local official in Luoyang. Who does not need to register a household? How can I give way to the censor like an ordinary official?"

Emperor Xiaowen listened and said with a smile: "Luoyang is the capital which belongs to me, and you should split your way. From now on, you can go separately on your own way!"

jurisdiction

n. 司法权

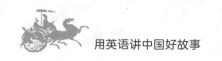

感恩图报

【释义】感激别人的恩情而设法报答。

【出处】《寄欧阳舍人书》:"其感与报,宜若何而图之。"

春秋时候,吴国有名大将军叫伍子胥,文武双全,有勇有谋,常让敌人闻风丧胆。有一次,伍子胥率军攻打郑国,郑定公传令下去:"谁能够让伍子胥退兵,就能得到重赏。"一连三天没人问津。第四天早上,有个年轻的渔夫表示,他有办法让伍子胥不来攻打郑国,而且不用一兵一卒。

郑定公将信将疑,答应让渔夫试试。渔夫带上自己划船的桨,直奔吴国兵营,去找伍子胥。他一边唱着歌,一边敲着那把船桨,打着节奏,唱道:"芦中人,芦中人;渡过江,谁的恩?宝剑上,七星文;还给你,带在身。你今天,得意了;可记得,渔丈人?"

伍子胥看到渔夫手中的船桨,大吃一惊,马上问道:"年轻人,你是谁呀?"渔夫回答说:"你没看到我手里拿的船桨吗?我父亲就是靠这根船桨过日子,他还用这根船桨救了你呀。"

伍子胥一听:"我想起来了!以前我逃难的时候,有一个渔夫救过我,我一直想报答他呢!原来你是他的儿子,你怎么来这里呢?"

渔夫说:"还不是因为你们吴国要来攻打我们郑国,我们这些打渔的人通通被叫到这里。我们的国君郑定公说:'只要谁能够请伍将军退兵,不来攻打郑国,我就重赏谁!'希望伍将军看在我死去的父亲曾经救过您的份上,不要来攻打郑国,也让我回去能得到一些奖赏。"

伍子胥带着感激的语气说:"因为你父亲救了我,我才能够活着当上大将军。我怎么会忘记他救命之恩,不感恩图报呢?"说完就下令退兵。郑定公也兑现了自己的承诺,奖给渔夫一百里土地。

Feel Grateful and Plan to Repay It

Paraphrase

Try to pay back the kindness of others out of gratitude.

Source

A Letter to Ouyang Sheren: How can I express my gratitude and repay the kindness?

During the Spring and Autumn Period, there was a famous general Wu Zixu in Wu State. He was a master of both pen and sword. He was courageous and resourceful, who often frightened the enemy. Once, Wu Zixu led an army to attack Zheng State. Duke Ding of Zheng ordered, "Who let Wu Zixu withdraw his troops will receive a big reward." For three days no one responded. On the morning of the fourth day, a young fisherman said that he had a way to keep Wu Zixu from attacking Zheng State without using a single soldier.

Not fully convinced, Duke Ding agreed to let the fisherman have a try. The fisherman took his oars and went straight to the Wu State's military camp to find Wu Zixu. As he sang, he beat the oar and sang in rhythm, "The people in the reed, the people in the reed; cross the river, whose grace? On the sword, the seven stars; give it back to you, and take it with you. You are **triumphant** today; do

triumphant

adj. 高奏凯歌的，大获全胜的

you still remember the fisherman?"

Wu Zixu saw the fisherman's oars, startled, and immediately asked, "Young man, who are you?" The fisherman answered, "Don't you see the oars in my hand? It was these oars that my father lived on, and it was these oars that saved your life, too."

Hearing the fisherman's words, Wu Zixu said, "I remember! Once when I was running away, a fisherman saved me. I always wanted to repay him. So you are his son. Why did you come here?"

The fisherman said, "It is because Wu State is going to attack Zheng State. All fishermen have been called here. Our Duke Ding said anyone who can ask you not to attack Zheng State will get a big reward. Since my late father saved you before, I hope you would not attack Zheng State, and I can also get some reward when I return."

Wu said in a grateful tone, "Because your father saved me, I was able to live and become a general. How could I forget his kindness for saving my life and not be grateful for it?" Then he ordered the troops to withdraw. Duke Ding also fulfilled his promise by awarding the fishermen 100 *li* of land.

观棋不语

【释义】 看别人下棋时不要说话。比喻静观其变，不发表自己意见；也比喻一个人有修养。

【出处】《奕喻》："后有招予观弈者，终日默坐而已。"

钱大昕是清代史学家、汉学家，饮誉海内外的著名学者。年轻时聪明好学，下得一手好棋。有一天，他到朋友家做客，看朋友和客人下棋，客人棋艺一般，经常出些臭棋，把一旁看棋的钱大昕急得够呛，不仅笑话客人不会走棋，还不停地指点客人该如何如何，客人非常扫兴，又不好说什么。

见此情形，钱大昕的朋友让钱大昕和客人对弈一盘。钱大昕也毫不推辞，就与客人对弈起来。客人请他执黑先走，他也毫不客气，心里很是瞧不起客人。

前几手客人的布局很是平常，钱大昕更加看不起他。可几手下来，客人的棋子像是变戏法似的，成了一张密不透风的网，将钱大昕的黑子紧紧围住，杀得他走投无路。钱大昕把自己认为的高招都用上了，也无法脱身，最终客人赢了他13个子，钱大昕输得心服口服，满脸羞愧。

从此以后，钱大昕看人下棋时，再也不多言多语，而是默默地观看，细心揣摩走棋的每一步，不仅棋艺得到提升，自身的修养也一同提高。

Keep Silent While Watching the Chess Game

❖ Paraphrase

Don't talk while watching others playing chess. It is a metaphor of watching the changes without expressing one's own opinions; it is also used to describe a person who is cultivated.

❖ Source

Yiyu: When I was invited to watch others playing chess thereafter, I just sat and watched in silence.

Qian Daxin was a historian and **sinologist** in the Qing Dynasty, and a well-known scholar at home and abroad. When he was young, he was smart and eager to learn, and he was good at playing chess. One day, he paid a visit to a friend, and watched his friend playing chess with a guest. The guest seemed not to be so good at playing chess, and often made some bad moves. Daxin was anxious seeing this. He not only laughed at the guest's chess skills, but also constantly gave advice to him. The guest was very disappointed, but didn't know what to say.

Seeing this, Qian Daxin's friend asked Qian Daxin to play chess with his guest. Qian Daxin didn't hesitate to agree and played with the guest. The guest asked him to go

sinologist

n. 汉学家

first, and he also agreed without showing any politeness. He looked down upon the guest a lot.

The layout of the first few moves of the guest was very ordinary, so Qian Daxin looked down on him even more. But with a few more moves, the guest's chess pieces seemed to be **conjured**, and became an airtight net that tightly surrounded Qian Daxin's black pieces, leaving him in a desperate situation. Qian Daxin used all the tricks, but couldn't find a way out. In the end, the guest won by 13 pieces of Qian Daxin. Qian Daxin was sincerely convinced of the loss and was ashamed of himself.

From then on, when Qian Daxin watched others playing chess, he no longer talked much about the chess, but watched silently, and tried to figure out every move of the game. Not only did he improve his chess skills, he also improved his **self-cultivation**.

conjure

v. 变戏法

self-cultivation

n. 自我修养

过门不入

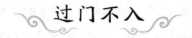

【释义】路过家门却不进去。形容恪尽职守，公而忘私。
【出处】《孟子·离娄下》："禹稷当平世，三过其门而不入。"

距今约 4,000 年前，尧、舜在位的时候，黄河流域经常发生大洪水，庄稼淹了，房屋毁了，人们无家可归。尧帝召集部落首领开会，商讨治水办法。大家公推鲧去治水。

鲧花了近 10 年的时间，用水来土挡的办法，造堤筑坝，结果并不理想，遇到更大的洪水，冲毁了堤坝，反而灾情更重。舜接替尧当部落联盟首领以后，认为鲧治水不力，就免了鲧的职，派他人来治水，却也见效甚微。于是有人推荐鲧的儿子禹。

禹从小发誓，一定要继承父亲的事业，治服洪水。他接到任务后，吸取父亲治水失败的教训，亲自带人跋山涉水，考察水流的源头和全程，并在重要的地方做上记号，便于将来治水时参考。

通过实地考察，禹了解到只用堵的方法治水是不行的，应该用开渠排水、疏通河道的办法，把洪水引到大海中去。他身先士卒，和老百姓一起劳动，戴着箬帽，拿着锹子，带头挖土、挑土，手脚都磨出了老茧。为了治水，他常年在外奔波，直到 30 多岁才结婚，新婚第四天，就上了治水工地。他的儿子长到 10 多岁，也没有见过父亲一面。传说禹有三次带人治水时路过自家门前，听见孩子的哭声，也没有进去看看。至今，乡间还流传着这样的歌谣：一过家门听骂声，二过家门听笑声，三过家门捎口讯，治平洪水转家中。这体现了大禹的事业心和责任感。禹三过家门不入的事传遍了各地，人们都很受感动。

禹治水有功，被推选为舜的接班人。舜死后，禹继任部落联盟首领。后来，大禹的儿子启创建了我国第一个奴隶制国家——夏朝，因此，后人也称他为夏禹。

Pass by the House Without Entering It

Paraphrase

Pass by one's own house but won't enter it. This idiom is used to describe people who are dedicated to his duties and forget about personal matters.

Source

Lilou II, Mencius: Yu and Houji lived in the peaceful era, and they passed by their homes three times but did not enter it.

About 4,000 years ago, during the reign of Yao and Shun, there were frequent floods in the Yellow River area. Crops were flooded, houses were destroyed, and people were left homeless. Emperor Yao had a meeting with **tribal** leaders to discuss ways to control the waters. Everyone recommended Gun to control the waters.

It took Gun for nearly ten years to build dams to defend against floods. The result was not satisfactory. In the case of greater floods, the dams were destroyed, and the disaster was worse. After Shun succeeded Yao as the leader of the tribal **alliance**, he thought that Gun was not effective in water control, so he relieved Gun of his position and sent others to control the waters, but also got little effect. So someone recommended Gun's son, Yu.

tribal
adj. 部落的，部族的

alliance
n. 联盟，同盟

Yu vowed from an early age that he must carry on his father's work to control the floods. After receiving the task, Yu learned from his father's failure to control the water, and led people to cross the mountains and rivers to carefully study the source and the water system, and mark important places for reference in future water control.

Through on-site studies, Yu learned that it is impossible to control the floods only by blocking up the water. Instead, people should build channels and divert the floods into the sea. He took the lead to work with the people, wearing a hat, holding a shovel, digging and picking soil, and his hands and feet were thickly **callused**. In order to control the waters, he traveled all year round and didn't get married until he was in his 30s. On the fourth day after his wedding, he went to the water control construction site. His son hadn't seen his father until he was over ten. It is said that for three times when Yu was leading people to control the floods, he passed by his own house and heard his child crying, but he did not go in the door to have a look. Up to now, there is still a song in the country: the first time passing by the house, curses were heard; the second time passing by the house, the laughter was heard, and the third time, a message was sent that "Not going home until the flood is controlled". These four lines reflect Yu's **dedication** and sense of responsibility. The story of Yu's controlling over floods spread everywhere, and people were very moved.

Yu was chosen as Shun's successor for his work

callused
adj. 起老茧的，有茧子的

dedication
n. 献身，奉献

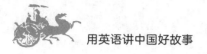

in controlling the floods. After the death of Shun, Yu succeeded the leader of the tribal alliance. Later, Qi, the son of Yu, founded the Xia Dynasty, the first slavery country in China. Therefore, later generations also called him Xia Yu.

邯郸学步

【释义】比喻一味地模仿别人，不仅没学到本事，反而把原来的长处也丢了。

【出处】《汉书·叙传上》："昔有学步于邯郸者，曾未得其仿佛，又复失其故步，遂匍匐而归耳。"

　　战国时期，燕国有个少年，听说赵国邯郸人走路的姿势特别优美，于是不顾路途遥远，特地到邯郸去学习当地人走路的姿势。

　　一进邯郸城，他就发现路上的行人，无论老少男女，走起路来都分外优雅，举手投足都带有赵国首都百姓特有的风度。他觉得不虚此行，应该好好学习。

　　学了几天，不见有长进，他想一定是自己走路的习惯太顽固了，只有把原来在燕国养成的走路习惯彻底忘掉，才有可能学到新的走法。

　　他决心从头学起，怎么抬脚，怎么跨步，怎么摆手，怎么扭腰，都机械地模仿邯郸人的姿态去做。过一段时间，新的走法没有学会，原来的走法也忘记了。当他返回燕国的时候，连路也不会走了，只好爬着回去。

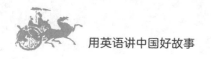

Learn to Walk in Handan

Paraphrase

It is used to describe people who blindly imitate others. Not only did he learn nothing, but also lost his original strength.

Source

Afterword and Family History, Part I, *Book of Han*: Once there was a man who learned to walk in Handan. The new way of walking was not learned and the original way of walking was forgotten. As a result he had to crawl back.

During the Warring States Period, there was a young man in Yan State. He heard that people in Handan of Zhao State had a particularly graceful walking posture. So regardless of the long distance, he went to Handan to learn the walking posture of the locals.

As soon as he entered Handan, he found that the pedestrians on the road, whether young or old, men or women, walked very elegantly, with the unique **demeanor** of the residents of the capital. He felt that this trip was worthwhile and he should study hard.

After studying for a few days, he didn't see any improvement. He thought that his old walking habit was too stubborn. Only by completely forgetting the old

demeanor

n. 行为，举止

walking habit that he had cultivated in Yan State could he learn a new way of walking.

He decided to learn from the beginning: how to lift the foot, how to step, how to move the hand, and how to twist the waist, and mechanically imitate the gestures of Handan people. After a period of time, the new way of walking was not learned and the original way of walking was forgotten. When he returned to Yan State, he could not even walk, so he had to crawl back.

狐假虎威

【释义】比喻仰仗或倚仗别人的权势来欺压、恐吓人。

【出处】《战国策·楚策一》："虎不知兽畏己而走也，以为畏狐也。"

老虎是森林之王，野兽们都怕它，看见它就躲得远远的。

老虎逮住了一只狐狸，正要下口，狐狸说话了："你竟敢吃我！你不知道我是天帝派来管理森林野兽的吗？今天你要吃了我，你就违抗了天帝的天命！"

老虎从鼻子里"哼"了一声，心想，谁不知道我才是百兽之王，今天怎么又冒出个百兽之长呢？

狐狸从老虎的表情看出它内心的疑惑，就说："你要不信，咱们试试。我在前面走，你在后面跟着看，看看森林中大大小小的野兽，有哪个见了我不逃跑远远的？"

老虎想，对啊，口说为虚，眼见为实，我就跟在它后边，它还能作假骗我不成！它要是骗了我，也逃不出我的手掌心。

于是，狐狸在前，老虎在后，向着森林深处走去。狐狸知道老虎在背后，不用担心别的野兽会来偷袭，就故意摆出一副不可一世的架势，大摇大摆地走着。老虎为了看个清楚，又怕狐狸耍小心眼逃跑了，就一步不离地紧跟后面。果然，小兔子、小猴子吓得没命地逃了，野猪和恶狼撒腿溜了；连凶猛的金钱豹和独角犀牛也远远地躲进树丛里了。狐狸更加神气，胸脯挺得高高的，连肚子都腆了起来。傻里傻气的老虎还真的相信了，对狐狸佩服得五体投地。它做梦也不会想到，大大小小的野兽们是见了它自己，才没命地逃跑躲藏的，而不是怕狐狸。

The Fox Exploits the Tiger's Might

❖ Paraphrase

It is used to describe someone who rely on the power of others to oppress and intimidate other people.

❖ Source

Strategies of Chu I, Strategies of the Warring States: The tiger didn't know it was the sight of himself that led the beasts to run, rather than for fear of the fox.

The tiger was the king of the forest. The wild beasts were afraid of him, and they hid far away when they saw him.

The tiger caught a fox and was about to bite when the fox said, "How dare you eat me! Don't you know that I was sent by the Emperor of Heaven to govern the beasts of the forest? If you eat me today, you will disobey the **mandate** of Heaven!"

The tiger **snorted** from his nose, thinking, "Everyone knows doesn't know I'm the king of beasts. How come there's another ruler of the beasts?"

The fox read the doubt in the tiger's face and said, "If you don't believe me, let's have a try. I will go on ahead, and you follow me. Let's see the wild animals, large and small, who will not run away when they see me?"

mandate
n. 授权

snort
v. 喷鼻息，哼

The tiger thought, "That was right. Seeing is believing. I will follow him, and he can not cheat me! If he lied to me, he would not escape from me."

So the fox went in front the tiger, and went deeper into the forest. The fox knew that the tiger was behind him and did not have to worry about other wild animals coming to attack him, so he deliberately put on an arrogant posture and swagged along. In order to see clearly, and in case that fox would play a trick and run away, the tiger followed very closely behind the fox. Sure enough, rabbits and monkeys were scared to death and ran away desperately; wild boars and wolves ran away in fright; even the fierce leopard and the one-horned **rhinoceros** hid far away in the forest. The fox was even more proud, with a high chest and a stood out belly. The silly tiger believed in it and admired the fox to the utmost. He would not have dreamed that it was the sight of the tiger that led wild animals to run and hide, rather than for fear of the fox.

rhinoceros

n. 犀牛

成语故事

画龙点睛

【释义】比喻写文章或讲话时，在关键处用几句话点明实质，使内容更加生动传神。

【出处】《历代名画记·张僧繇》："金陵安乐寺四白龙不点眼睛，每云：'点睛即飞去。'"

张僧繇是南北朝时期著名的大画家，他特别善于画龙。有一年，梁武帝要张僧繇为金陵的安乐寺作画，在寺庙的墙壁上画四条金龙。他答应下来，仅用三天时间就画好了。这些龙画得栩栩如生，惟妙惟肖，活灵活现，简直就像真龙一样。

张僧繇画好后，吸引很多人前去观看，都称赞画得好，太逼真了。可人们走近一看，发现四条龙全都没有眼睛，感到遗憾，又大惑不解，纷纷请求画家把眼睛点上。张僧繇解释说："给龙点上眼睛并不难，但是点上了，龙就会飞走。"没人相信他的话，认为这样的解释很荒唐，还有人认为他在说谎，是为自己画不好眼睛狡辩。张僧繇被逼得没有办法，只好答应给龙"点睛"，但说好只给其中一条龙点睛，其余三条金龙要留在墙壁上。

这一天，在寺庙墙壁前有很多人围观，张僧繇当着众人的面，提起画笔，轻轻地给一条龙点上眼睛。奇怪的事情果然发生了，他刚点过第一条龙的眼睛，就见晴朗的天空突然乌云密布，狂风四起，雷鸣电闪，在雷电之中，刚刚被"点睛"的那条龙震破墙壁凌空而起，腾云驾雾，飞向天空。

过了一会，云散天晴，再看看墙上，只剩下了没有被点上眼睛的三条龙，而另外一条被"点睛"的龙不知去向了。人们被吓得目瞪口呆，一句话都说不出来了，这才相信张僧繇说的是真话。

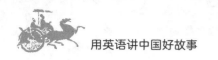

Add Eyes to a Dragon

Paraphrase

Use a few sentences to point out the essence of an article or a speech to make the content more vivid.

Source

Zhang Sengyao, Notes of Past Famous Paintings: There were four dragons painted on the walls of the Anle Temple in Jinling, but without eyes. Every time it is explained as "once painted the eyes, the dragon will fly away".

Zhang Sengyao was a famous painter in the Southern and Northern Dynasties. He was particularly good at drawing dragons. One year, Emperor Wu of Liang asked Zhang Sengyao to paint four golden dragons on the walls of the Anle Temple in Jinling. He agreed and finished the paintings in only three days. These dragons were drawn quite vividly, just like real dragons.

After Zhang Sengyao finished the painting, many people were attracted to watch it. They all praised the painting for being so realistic. But when people came closer, they found that none of the four dragons had eyes. They were regretful and puzzled, and they asked the painter to put their eyes on. Zhang Sengyao explained,

"It's not difficult to put the eyes on the dragon, but if I do so, the dragon will fly away." No one believed his words, thinking this explanation was absurd, and some people thought he was lying because he was bad at drawing the eyes. Zhang Sengyao had no choice but to agree to give the dragon a "finish touch", but he agreed that only one of the dragons would be given the eyes, and the other three golden dragons would remain on the wall.

On this day, there were many onlookers in front of the temple wall. Zhang Sengyao raised his paintbrush and lightly drew the eyes on a dragon. Strange things happened as expected. When he just finished painting the first dragon's eyes, the sunny sky suddenly turned cloudy, and gusty winds came. In the thunder and lightning, the dragon just painted with eyes shattered the wall and flew to the sky.

After a while, the sky cleared. On the wall, there were only three dragons left without eyes, and the one with eyes disappeared. People were so stunned that they couldn't say a word, and then they believed that Zhang Sengyao was telling the truth.

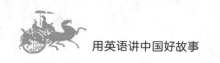

画蛇添足

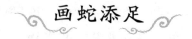

【释义】画蛇时给蛇添上脚,后比喻做了多余的事,非但无益,反而害事。

【出处】《战国策·齐策二》:"蛇固无足,子安能为之足?"

古代楚国,有一人家祭祀祖宗。完毕后,把祭祀用的一壶酒,赏给帮忙办事的人喝。人多酒少,很难分配。与其每人喝一点,还不如让一个人喝个痛快。大家在一起想办法,谁都想喝这壶酒。

有人建议来个画蛇比赛,每个人在地上画一条蛇,谁画得快,这壶酒就归他喝。大家都认为这个方法好,每个人折一个树枝,听到开始的指令后,同时开始画。

有个人画得最快,转眼之间,把蛇画好了。他抓过酒壶,得意地看看同伴,心想,他们画得真慢,便洋洋得意地说:"我再给蛇画上几只脚,你们也赶不上我。"于是,他左手提着酒壶,右手给蛇画起脚来。

正在他给蛇画脚的时候,另一个人已经画好了。那人一把夺过酒壶,咕咚咕咚把酒喝下去了,还嘲笑说:"你见过蛇有脚吗?你画的根本就不是蛇。我才是第一个画好蛇的人,酒应当归我喝。"

画蛇添足的人无话可说,只好咽着唾沫,看别人喝酒,心里懊恼不已。

Add Feet When Drawing a Snake

Paraphrase

Add feet to a snake when drawing. It is used to describe people who do unnecessary things, which is not only useless, but harmful.

Source

Strategies of Qi II, Strategies of the Warring States: Snakes have no feet. How can you put feet on it?

In ancient Chu State, there was a family offering sacrifices to their ancestors. After it, they gave a pot of wine used for the sacrifice to the people who helped with the affairs. There were too many people but too little wine, so it is difficult to **distribute** the wine. It was better to give one a good drink than to each a sip. Everyone tried to find a way. Nobody didn't want to drink the wine.

Someone suggested that they have a snake painting competition. Everyone drew a snake on the ground. Whoever drew the fastest would drink the wine. The others thought that was a good idea. Each person broke off a branch, and began to draw at the same time on hearing the starting command.

One man was the fastest, and in a twinkling of an eye, he finished drawing the snake. He grabbed the pot and

distribute

v. 分配

looked **gloatingly** at his companions. They were drawing very slowly, he thought, so he said triumphantly, "I'll add some feet to the snake, and you won't be able to catch up with me." So he took the pot in his left hand and drew feet for the snake with his right hand.

While he was drawing feet for the snake, another man had already finished. The man grabbed the pot and drank the wine. He laughed and said, "Have you ever seen a snake with feet? What you paint isn't a snake at all. I was the first to draw a snake, and the wine should belong to me."

The man who drew feet to the snake had nothing to say but swallowed his **saliva** and watched the other man drink the wine, feeling very frustrated.

gloatingly
adv. 沾沾自喜的

saliva
n. 唾液

讳疾忌医

【释义】隐瞒疾病，不愿医治。比喻怕人批评而掩饰自己的缺点和错误。

【出处】《周子通书·过》："今人有过，不喜人规，如讳疾而忌医，宁灭其身而无悟也。"

扁鹊是战国时期一位名医，他真实的姓名叫"秦越人"，因其出生中医世家，医术高超，人们以上古神话中黄帝时期的神医"扁鹊"来称呼他。

有一天，他去见蔡桓公，见桓公气色不好，提醒说："大王，您得病了，现在病在皮肤表层，很快就能治愈。"桓公听了，笑着说："我没有病。"扁鹊走后，桓公对身边的人说："你们看这些医生，眼里都是病人，总想着给没有病的人治病，治好了证明自己医术高明。"

十天后，扁鹊又去看望桓公，一见面，就着急地说："大王，您的病加重了，从皮肤发展到肌肉里了，可得抓紧治啊！"桓公很不高兴。

又过了十天，扁鹊再去看望桓公，大惊失色，紧张地催促说："大王，您的病更重了，已经转移到肠胃里了，不赶快医治，是有生命危险的！"桓公更不高兴了。

又过了十天，扁鹊再一次去拜望桓公，只远远地看上一眼，转身就走。桓公见状，很是奇怪，就让人追问扁鹊。

扁鹊说："病在皮肤表层的时候，可以用热敷；病在肌肉里，可以用针灸；病到肠胃里，可以吃汤药；现在大王已经病入骨髓里，只能听天由命，我也没有办法能救大王了。"

五天以后，桓公浑身疼痛，赶忙派人去请扁鹊，扁鹊却早已经逃到邻国去了。没过几天，桓公就病死了。

Conceal the Illness from the Doctor

Paraphrase

Conceal the illness and refuse to treat it. It refers to people who cover up his shortcomings and mistakes for fear of being criticized.

Source

Guo, Zhouzi Tongshu：Now someone has made a mistake, but is unwilling to listen to others' opinions, just like the man who concealed his illness and avoided the treatment, and wouldn't realize the truth even at the cost of self-destruction.

Bian Que was a famous doctor in the Warring States Period. His real name was Qin Yueren. He was born into a family of traditional Chinese medicine doctors with excellent medical skills, so he was named Bian Que, after a genius doctor of the Yellow Emperor era in ancient **mythology**.

One day, he went to see Duke Huan of Cai, and he didn't look good. Bian Que reminded him, "Your Majesty, you are ill. Now the virus is on the surface of your skin, and it will soon be cured." Hearing this, Duke Huan laughed and said, "I am not ill." After Bian Que left, Duke Huan said to the people around him, " Look at these

conceal
v. 隐藏，隐瞒

mythology
n. 神话

doctors. People are all patients in their eyes. They always want to treat those who are not sick to prove that they are highly skilled in medicine."

Ten days later, Bian Que went to see Duke Huan again. When they met, he said anxiously, "Your Majesty, your illness is getting worse. It has developed from your skin to your muscles. You should treat it as soon as possible." Duke Huan was very unhappy.

After another ten days, Bian Que went to see Duke Huan again. He was alarmed and urged him nervously, saying, "Your majesty, your illness has become more serious and it has moved to your stomach. If you don't get medical treatment soon, you will be in danger." Duke Huan was even more unhappy.

Ten days later, Bian Que went to see Duke Huan again. He only took a look at him from a distance, then turned and went away. When Duke Huan saw this, he was confused and let people ask Bian Que for the reason.

Bian Que said, "When the disease is on the surface of the skin, you can use hot **compress**; When the disease is in the muscles, you can use acupuncture; When the disease is in the stomach, you can take decoctions; Now His Majesty has become very sick and can only obey his fate. I can't save him."

Five days later, Duke Huan was aching all over, so he sent for Bian Que. Bian Que had already fled to a neighboring state. A few days later, Duke Huan died of illness.

compress
n.（止血、减痛等的）敷布

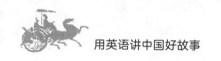

解铃还须系铃人

【释义】谁引起的问题就由谁来解决。

【出处】《林间集》：一日法眼问大众曰："虎项下金铃，何人解得？"泰钦曰："大众何不道：'系者解得。'"

南唐高僧法眼，是中国佛教史上禅门五宗之一——"法眼宗"的始祖，住在金陵清凉寺，也就是今天南京清凉山公园的清凉寺。

当时，有一位泰钦法灯禅师，也住在清凉寺里，他性格豪放，平时不拘小节，大大咧咧，寺内和尚大多看不起他，唯独住持法眼禅师对他非常尊重。

有一次，法眼在讲经说法之后，向寺内的和尚们问了一个问题："老虎的脖子上系着一串铃铛，谁能把它解下来？"

大家面面相觑，都回答不出来。这时法灯刚巧走过来，法眼用同样的问题问法灯，法灯不假思索地答道："那个把铃铛系到老虎脖子上的人能够解下来。"

法眼十分满意法灯的回答，对大家说："你们可不能看不起他啊！"后来个故事就以"解铃还需系铃人"的成语流传下来，比喻谁惹出来的事情，还请谁去解决。

Who Tied the Bell Should Untie It

❈ **Paraphrase**

Whoever causes the problem should solve the problem.

❈ **Source**

Linjianji: One day, Fayan asked the monks, "A tiger wears gold bells around its neck. Who can take it off?" Tai Qin said, "Who tied the bells can untie it."

Fayan, an **eminent** monk in the Southern Tang Dynasty, was the ancestor of one of the five Zen sects in the history of Chinese Buddhism—the Fayan School, one of the five schools of Zen in the history of Buddhism in China. He lived in Qingliang Temple in Jinling, which is today the Qingliang Temple in Qingliang Mountain Park in Nanjing.

eminent
adj. 卓越的，显赫的

At that time, there was a Zen master Tai Chin Fadeng, who also lived in the Qingliang Temple. He had a bold and **unrestrained** personality and was careless in daily life. Most of the monks in the temple looked down upon him, but the abbot Fayan showed him great respect.

unrestrained
adj. 不加制约的

Once, after giving a lecture, Fayan asked the monks in the temple a question, "A tiger has a bunch of bells around its neck. Who can take it off?"

Everyone looked at each other but could not answer. Fayan asked Fadeng the same question. Without thinking, Fadeng answered, "The man who tied the bells to the tiger's neck can take them off."

Fayan was very satisfied with the answer of Fadeng and said to everyone, "You can't look down upon him!" Later, a story was passed down as the idiom "Who tied the bell should untie it", as a metaphor for who causes the problem should solve the problem.

惊弓之鸟

【释义】被弓箭吓怕了的鸟不容易安定。比喻受过惊吓的人碰到一点动静就非常害怕。

【出处】《晋书·王鉴传》:"黩武之众易动,惊弓之鸟难安。"

战国时期,魏国有一名神箭手叫更羸,箭术非常高超,可以说是百发百中。一天他陪魏王一起散步,看见天空中有几只大雁飞过,就对魏王说:"我不用箭,只用弓,就可以把鸟射下来。"魏王不相信,更羸说:"我试给你看。"

不一会儿,有一只大雁从东方飞来,只见更羸举弓拉弦,随着"嘣"的一声弦响,大雁从空中掉了下来。

魏王大吃一惊,赞赏道:"想不到你箭术高超到这样地步,竟有这样的本领!"

更羸说:"向大王您报告,不是我的箭术高明,而是这只大雁受过箭伤。"

魏王更加好奇了:"大雁远在天上,你怎么知道它受过箭伤?"

更羸说:"这只大雁飞得很慢,叫声悲凉。据我经验,飞得很慢是因为体内有伤;叫声悲凉是因为离开了雁群。这只大雁惊魂未定,突然听到弦响的声音,就拼命向高处飞,一使劲,伤口裂开,就掉了下来。"

魏王检查掉下来的大雁,果然如更羸所说。

用英语讲中国好故事

A Bird Startled by a Bow

Paraphrase

A bird frightened by a bow and arrow cannot easily settle down. It is used to describe people who have been frightened before will easily get frightened later.

Source

The Biography of Wang Jian, Book of Jin: An army that abuses force is prone to **impulse**, and a bird frightened by a bow can hardly settle down.

impulse
n. 冲动

During the Warring States Period, there was a skillful archer named Geng Lei in Wei State. His skill was so excellent that he hit the target every time. One day he was taking a walk with the King of Wei. When he saw some wild geese flying by in the sky, he said to the King, "I don't need arrows. I can shoot down birds with only a bow." The King of Wei didn't believe him, so Geng Lei said, "I'll show you."

After a while, a wild goose came flying from the east. Geng Lei raised his bow and pulled the strings. With a bang, the goose fell down from the sky.

The King of Wei was **astounded** and praised, "I never expected that you would have such good shooting skills!"

Geng Lei said, "I'd like to tell Your Majesty that it is

astounded
adj. 感到震惊的

not my shooting skills are good, but that this wild goose has been wounded by an arrow."

The King of Wei became even more curious, "The wild goose is far away in the sky. How do you know it was wounded by an arrow?"

Geng Lei said, "This goose flies very slowly and has a sad cry. According to my experience, it flies very slowly because of the wound and the cry is sad because it has left the geese. The wild goose is in shock and suddenly heard the string. With the loud sound, he flew to a high place desperately, and with a hard effort, the wound split and it fell off."

The King of Wei checked the fallen geese, and it was just as Geng Lei said.

井底之蛙

【释义】井底的青蛙认为天只有井口那么大。比喻见识短浅的人。

【出处】《庄子·秋水》:"井蛙不可以语于海者,拘于虚也。"

有一只青蛙长年住在一口废井里,它对自己生活的小天地满意极了,一有机会就要当众吹嘘一番。

有一天,青蛙在井边遇见一只从海里来的大龟。青蛙热情地对海龟说:"你看,我住在这里多快乐呀!高兴了,就在井栏边跳跃一阵;疲倦了,就回到井里睡一觉。有时我只露出头和嘴巴,把全身泡在水里,特别享受;或者在井底软绵绵的泥浆里散散步,也很舒适。看看那些虾和蝌蚪,谁也比不上我的生活。而且,我是这个井里的主人,我爱怎么着就怎么着,自由自在,你不想进来看看我的家吗?"

海龟听了青蛙的话,倒真想进去看看。但它的左脚还没有整个伸进井里,右脚又被井口卡住了。海龟只好慢慢地退出来,问青蛙:"你听说过大海吗?"青蛙摇摇头。

海龟说:"大海水天茫茫,无边无际,用千里不能形容它的辽阔,用万丈不能表明它的深度。传说四千多年以前,大禹做国君的时候,十年九涝,海水没有加深;三千多年以前,商汤统治的年代,八年七旱,海水也不见减少。海是这样大,以至时间的长短、旱涝的变化都不能使它的水量发生明显的变化。青蛙老弟呀,我就生活在大海中。你看,比起你这一眼废井、一坑浅水,哪个天地更开阔、哪个乐趣更大呢?"

青蛙听傻了,鼓着眼睛,半天合不拢嘴。

A Frog at the Bottom of a Well

❦ Paraphrase

The frog at the bottom of the well thinks the sky is only as big as the mouth of the well. It is a metaphor referring to short-sighted people.

❦ Source

Autumn Floods, Zhuangzi: One shouldn't talk about sea to the frog in the well, because its vision is limited by its small residence.

There was a frog who had lived in an abandoned well for many years. He was so happy with the little world he lived in that he would brag about it in public whenever he could.

One day, the frog met a big turtle at the well that came from the sea. The frog said to the turtle warmly, "Look, I am so happy to live here! When I am glad, I jump a little by the well fence; When I am tired, I go back to the well to sleep. Sometimes I only pop out my head and mouth, and soak my whole body in the water, enjoying it very much. Or I will take a walk in the soft mud at the bottom of a well and look at those shrimps and **tadpoles**. No one's life is better than mine. Besides, I am the master of this well, and I am free to do anything I like. Don't you want to

tadpole

n. 蝌蚪

come and see my well?"

After hearing what the frog said, the turtle really wanted to go in and took a look. But before his left foot could reach the well, his right foot got stuck in the mouth. The turtle had to withdraw slowly and asked the frog, "Have you heard of the sea?" The frog shook his head.

The turtle said, "The sea is vast and boundless. Thousands of miles cannot describe its vastness, and tens of thousands of meters cannot express its depth. Legend has it that more than four thousand years ago, when Great Yu was the king, there were floods in nine years out of ten and the sea water did not increase. More than three thousand years ago, in the era of Tang of Shang Dynasty, there were droughts in seven years out of eight and the sea water did not decrease. The sea is so big that even the length of time and the changes in drought and flood could not make any obvious changes in its water volume. Brother frog, I live in the ocean. Compared with your waste well and shallow water, which world is more open and which has more fun?"

On hearing the turtle's words, the frog was **dumbfounded**, with his eyes bulging and his mouth open for a long time.

dumbfounded
adj. 惊呆了的

九死一生

【释义】 形容经历极大危险而死里逃生。也形容处在生死关头,情况十分危急。

【出处】《离骚》:"虽九死其犹未悔。"

屈原,战国时期楚国人,政治家,中国文学史上的第一位爱国诗人、浪漫主义诗人。

屈原出生于楚国贵族家庭,自幼好学,有远大志向。早年得到楚怀王重用,辅佐楚怀王变法图强,联齐抗秦,楚国国力一度增强。后因小人诬陷,楚怀王疏远了屈原。在楚怀王、楚襄王当政期间,先后两次遭到流放。流放期间,屈原创作了中国最早的长篇抒情诗《离骚》,表达爱国忠心和自己的不平遭遇。在《离骚》里屈原写道:"亦余心之所善兮,虽九死其犹未悔。"其意思是说,这是我心中追求的东西,即使多次有死亡的危险也不后悔。诗人坚持自己的政治理想和人生追求,不惜牺牲自己的生命,也毫不退缩,勇往直前。

公元前278年,秦军攻破楚国国都。屈原满怀对国家和人民的无限深情,在绝望和悲愤之中,于同年5月投汨罗江而死,以身殉国。

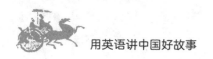

A Narrow Escape from Death

❖ **Paraphrase**

It is used to describe the escape from death after experiencing great danger or a life and death situation.

❖ **Source**

Li Sao: I still have no regrets although I would die many times.

Qu Yuan was a politician and statesman of Chu State during the Warring States Period. He was the first **patriotic** and romantic poet in the history of Chinese literature.

Qu Yuan was born in an **aristocratic** family of Chu State. He was studious and ambitious since his childhood. In his early years, he was put in an important position by King Huai of Chu and assisted King Huai in his political reform to strengthen Chu. He allied with Qi State and fought against Qin State. As a result, the strength of Chu State was once strengthened. Later, he was framed by the villain, and then King Huai **alienated** Qu Yuan. During the reign of King Huai and King Xiang of Chu, he was **exiled** twice. During his exile, Qu Yuan wrote China's first long lyric poem, *Li Sao*, to express his patriotic loyalty and his own grievances. In *Li Sao*, Qu Yuan had written, "I am still not regretful for what the ideal in my heart although

patriotic
adj. 爱国的
aristocratic
adj. 贵族的

alienate
v. 疏远
exile
v. 流放

I would die nine times." That is to say, for what I pursue in my heart, even though I have been in danger of dying many times, I will not regret it. The poet **adheres** to his own political ideal and life pursuit, and does not hesitate to sacrifice his own life.

In 278 BC, the Qin army broke through the capital of Chu State. Full of infinite affection for the country and the people, Qu Yuan, in despair and grief, suicided for his country in the Miluo River in May of the same year.

adhere

v. 坚持

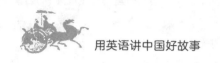

开天辟地

【释义】古代神话中说盘古氏开天辟地,从此才有人类。后来用"开天辟地"比喻创建前所未有的大业。

【出处】《补张灵·崔莹合传》:"此开天辟地第一吃紧事也。"

相传天地还没有形成以前,宇宙漆黑一片、混沌一团。它无边无沿,没有上下左右,也不分东南西北,样子好像一个浑圆的大鸡蛋。盘古在这里被孕育成人以后,睡了一万八千年。

有一天,盘古突然醒来,睁眼一看,漆黑一团,什么也看不见。盘古就拔下自己的一颗牙齿,把它变成威力巨大的神斧,抡起神斧向四周劈去。刹那间,天崩地裂,一阵巨响过后,这个大鸡蛋裂开了。其中一些轻而清的东西,慢慢上升变成了天空;另一些重而浊的东西,缓缓下沉变成了大地。从此,混沌不分的宇宙变成了天和地。

天地刚分开后,盘古站在大地之间,头顶着天,脚踩着地,不让天地再合拢起来。天每日增高一丈,地每日增厚一丈,盘古也每日长高一丈。这样又经过一万八千年,天高得不能再高,地深得不能再深,盘古自己也变成了九万里长的顶天立地的巨人,像一根柱子一样撑着天和地。

盘古开天辟地后,天地间只有他一个人。因为天地是他开辟出来的,所以他的情绪有什么变化,天地也跟着发生不同的变化。他高兴的时候天空晴朗,发怒的时候天空阴沉,哭泣的时候天空下雨,叹气的时候刮起狂风,呼出的气变成了风和云。他眨眨眼睛,天空出现闪电;他发出鼾声,空中响起雷声。盘古死后,左眼变成了太阳,右眼变成了月亮;头发和胡须变成了星星。他躺倒在地上,隆起的头部成为东岳泰山,朝天的脚成为西岳华山,

高挺的肚子成为中岳嵩山，两个肩胛成为南岳衡山和北岳恒山，头发和汗毛变成了树木和花草。后来，才有了传说中的远古帝王——三皇，即天皇、地皇和人皇。

Split Heaven and Earth Apart

❖ Paraphrase

According to ancient myths, human beings appeared after Pangu split heaven and earth apart. Later, this idiom is used as a metaphor for the creation of unprecedented undertakings.

❖ Source

Biographies of Zhang Ling and Cui Ying: This is the first priority since the split of heaven and earth.

Legend has it that before the world was created, the universe was dark and **chaotic**. It had no edge, no borders, and no directions. It looked like a big round egg. Pangu slept for 18,000 years since he was conceived in it.

chaotic

adj. 混乱的

One day, Pangu woke up suddenly, and when he opened his eyes, it was dark and he could see nothing. Pangu pulled off one of his teeth, turned it into a mighty magic axe, and swung it around. In an instant, the sky broke and the earth cracked. And after a loud noise, the big egg cracked. Some of the light and clear things slowly rose to become the sky; the other heavy and muddy things slowly sank and became the earth. Since then, the chaotic universe has become heaven and earth.

Immediately after the heaven and earth separated,

Pangu stood between them, with his head in the sky, his feet on the ground, not allowing them to close again. The sky rised by ten feet every day, the earth thickened by ten feet every day, and Pangu also grew by ten feet every day. In this way, after another 18,000 years, the sky couldn't be higher, and the earth couldn't be thicker. Pangu himself became a 90,000-*li*-long giant, supporting the sky and the earth like a pillar.

After the creation of the world by Pangu, he was the only one in the world. As he had created heaven and earth, they changed with Pangu's mood. When he was happy the sky was clear. When he was angry, it was dark. When he cried, it rained. When he sighed, there was a strong wind, and his breath became wind and cloud. When he blinked, there was lightning flashing in the sky; when he snored and there was thunder in the air. After his death, his left eye became the sun and his right eye became the moon. His hair and **whiskers** turned into stars. He lay down on the ground, and his uplifted head became Mount Tai in the east, his uplifted feet Mount Hua in the west, his erect belly Mount Song in the middle part, his two shoulders Mount Heng in the south and Mount Heng in the north, and his hair and hairs trees and flowers. Later, there was the **legendary** ancient emperors—the Three Emperors, namely Emperor of Heaven, Emperor of Earth and Emperor of Human.

whisker
n. 须，胡子

legendary
adj. 传说的

刻舟求剑

【释义】比喻死守教条，拘泥成法，固执不变通。
【出处】《吕氏春秋·察今》："舟止，从其所契者入水求之。"

战国时期，有个楚国人坐船过江。船到江心，突然一个浪头打来，船身摇晃不停，这人不小心，随身携带的一把宝剑滑落，他赶紧伸手去抓，可惜为时已晚，宝剑已全部落入江水里了。船上的人对此感到非常惋惜。丢剑的人一点却也不焦急慌张，而是掏出一把小刀，在船舷上刻了一道记号，对大家说："我的宝剑就是从这个地方落水的。"

大家面面相觑，不明白他为什么要这样做。

船靠岸后，那人立即在船上刻有记号的地方跳下去，在水里乱摸起来，嘴里念念有词："我的宝剑就是从这个地方落水的呀，我是在船沿刻了记号的。"

大家这才恍然大悟，又哭笑不得，纷纷说道："船一直在行进，而你掉入江中的宝剑，是不会跟着船在水里行走的，你怎能找得到剑呢？"

剑落入水中只会沉到水底，这是普通常识。船走远了，还要按照记号在船底下找那把之前掉下水的剑，真是愚蠢可笑。

Mark the Boat to Locate the Sword

Paraphrase

This means someone who are inflexible and stubbornly adhere to the **dogma**.

dogma

n. 教导

Source

Chajin, Lv's Spring and Autumn Annals: When the boat stopped, the man jumped into the water from the marked place to find the sword.

During the Warring States Period, a man from Chu State was crossing a river by boat. When the boat reached the middle of the river, a wave came and the boat shook uncontrollably. The man was not careful and the sword he was carrying slipped into the river. He reached out to catch it, but it was too late. People on board felt very sorry for this. The person who lost the sword was not anxious at all. Instead, he took out a small knife and carved a mark on the side of the boat, saying to everyone, "My sword fell into the water from this place."

Everyone looked at each other, wondering why he had done that.

As soon as the boat reached the shore, the man jumped into the water from the marked place, **fumbling** in the water and muttering to himself, "This is where my

fumble

v. 胡乱摸找（某物）

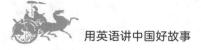

sword fell into the water. It was at the edge of the boat where I marked."

Everyone suddenly realized what happened and didn't know how to react. They all said, "The ship has been moving, and the sword fell into the river will not follow the ship in the water. How can you find the sword?"

A sword falling into the water will only sink to the bottom, which is common sense. The boat was far away and it is **ridiculous** to find the sword that fell into the water according to the mark under the boat.

ridiculous

adj. 荒谬的，荒唐的

滥竽充数

【释义】不会吹竽的人混在会吹竽的队伍里充数。比喻无本领的冒充有本领，次货冒充好货。

【出处】《韩非子·内储说上》："南郭处士请为王吹竽，宣王说（悦）之。"

战国时期，齐国有位国君叫齐宣王，喜欢音乐，特别喜欢听竽乐合奏，有一个300人的乐队为他演奏。

有个南郭先生，既不会吹竽，也不懂音乐，听说齐宣王喜欢听合奏，觉得有机可乘，可以混口饭吃。他向齐宣王毛遂自荐，吹嘘说："大王啊，我是吹竽的高手，听过我吹竽的人没有不被感动的，就是鸟兽听了也会翩翩起舞，花草听了也会合着节拍摆动。我听说大王您喜爱竽乐，我愿意把自己的绝技献给大王，让大王您高兴。"齐宣王听后非常开心，马上请他加入那支300人的吹竽乐队中。

从那以后，南郭先生就混在300人的乐队里给齐宣王吹竽，他摇头晃脑，装着十分投入和陶醉的样子，其实他的竽一点儿声音也没出，就这样靠着蒙骗混过了一天又一天，不劳而获地拿着丰厚的薪水，过着体面的生活，心里极为得意。

好景不长，齐宣王死后，他的儿子齐湣王继位。齐湣王也爱听吹竽，但他喜欢听独奏，于是发布了一道命令，让300个乐师一个一个轮流地吹竽给他听。南郭先生知道混不下去了，急得像热锅上的蚂蚁，惶惶不可终日。他思来想去，觉得三十六计走为上计，连夜收拾行李逃走了。

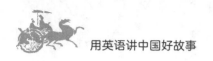

Pretend to Play the *Yu* to Get by

Paraphrase

People who don't know how to play the *yu* is in a team that can play the *yu*. It is a metaphor for an incompetent person who pretends to be competent, and a inferior product pretends to be a good product.

Source

The Upper Series of Inner Congeries of Sayings, Han Feizi: Nanguo offered to play the *yu* for the King, and King Xuan was very pleased.

During the Warring States Period, a monarch in Qi State was called King Xuan of Qi. He liked music, especially the music of *yu*. There was a 300-member band played for him.

There was a man called Nanguo, who could neither play the *yu* nor understand music. He heard that King Xuan liked listening to concert, and thought that he had the opportunity to earn a living on a free riding. He **recommended** himself to King Xuan and **boasted**, "My lord, I am a master player of *yu*. No one was not moved after they had heard me playing the *yu*. Even the birds and beasts will dance when they listen to it, and the flowers and plants will also move in rhythm. I heard that you love

recommend
v. 推荐
boast
v. 自夸

music of *yu*. My king, I am willing to dedicate my **stunts** to you, to make you happy." King Xuan was very pleased after hearing this, and immediately invited him to join the 300-member band.

Since then, Nanguo had been in the 300-member band to play the *yu* to King Xuan. He shook his head around and pretended to be very engaged and **intoxicated**. In fact, his *yu* didn't make a sound, and he was fooling around day by day. Getting a good salary for nothing, and living a decent life, he felt extremely proud.

The good times did not last long. After King Xuan died, his son King Min succeeded to the throne. King Min also liked to listen to the *yu*, but he liked to listen to solo. He issued an order that the 300 musicians needed to play the *yu* to him one by one. Nanguo knew that he couldn't fool around any longer. He was as anxious as an ant on a hot pot, and panicked all day long. Thinking it over and over, he decided that the best plan was to go, so he packed up and fled overnight.

stunt

n. 绝技，惊人的技艺

intoxicated

adj. 陶醉的

101

老马识途

【释义】老马认识路,比喻有经验的人能起引导的作用。
【出处】《韩非子·说林上》:"乃放老马而随之。遂得道。"

春秋时期,北方的山戎国入侵燕国,燕国派人向齐国求救。齐国国君齐桓公亲自率领大军去救燕国,把山戎国的军队逼进了深山荒林,不仅打败了入侵者,还把敌人掠夺的财物也夺了回来。

当他们得胜回朝,启程返回齐国时,却在深山密林中迷路了,怎么也走不出山谷。原来齐军来的时候是春天,山青水绿,道路容易辨认。返回时已是冬天,满山白雪皑皑,山路淹没不见,大军在崇山峻岭的山谷中转来转去,就是走不出去,照此下去,大军有困死山谷的危险。

齐桓公的大臣管仲猛然想起一件事,老马离家远了也能寻回家去,那么军中的马也应该有这个本能。于是他对齐桓公说:"老马有认路的本能,何不挑选几匹老马,让它们在前边带路,兴许可以走出去。"

齐桓公虽然将信将疑,但也无计可施,决定试一试再说,立即下令挑选几匹老马,放开缰绳,让它们在前边自由地走,队伍紧跟其后。只见几匹老马不慌不忙地走着,果然走出了山谷,回到了原来的路上,最终齐军顺利回国了。

An Old Horse Knows the Way

Paraphrase

It is a metaphor that an experienced person can play a guiding role.

Source

The Upper Series of Collected Persuasions, Han Feizi: So they let go of the old horse and followed behind it, and then found a way out.

During the Spring and Autumn Period, a country in the north called Shan Rong invaded Yan State, and Yan State asked Qi State for help. Duke Huan of Qi led an army in person to save Yan State, and forced Shan Rong's army into the remote mountains and forests. Not only did he defeat the invaders, he also took back the property **plundered** by the enemy.

When they set off to return to Qi State, they got lost in the dense forests, and could not get out of the valley. It turned out that it was spring when Qi army came, and with green mountains and clear water the roads were easy to be identified. But it was winter when they returned. The mountains and paths were covered with snow. The army wandered about in the valleys, but could not get out. If it continued like this, the army was in danger of dying in the

plunder

v. 抢掠，掠夺

103

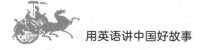

valleys.

It suddenly occurred to Guan Zhong, a minister of Qi State, that an old horse might be able to find its way home even when it was far away from home. So he suggested it to Duke Huan, "Old horses have the **instinct** of knowing the way. Why not choose some old horses and let them lead the way? Perhaps they can find a way out."

While skeptical of the suggestion, Duke Huan decided to give it a try. He ordered the soldiers to select some old horses and let go of their reins. The troops followed closely behind the horses. As expected, the old horses walked out of the valley and returned to the original road. Finally, the Qi army returned home smoothly.

instinct

n. 本能，天性

乐不思蜀

【释义】乐而忘返或乐而忘本。
【出处】《三国志·蜀书·后主传》:"此间乐,不思蜀。"

三国时期,刘备占据蜀地,建立蜀国。刘备死后,儿子刘禅继位,即蜀汉后主。刘禅小名阿斗,不思进取,即使有诸葛亮这样的名臣辅佐,也无济于事。公元263年,蜀国被魏国所灭,刘禅投降后,全家被迫迁到魏国国都洛阳。魏王封他为"安乐公"。

有一次,魏国大臣司马昭设宴招待刘禅,有意安排表演蜀国歌舞。刘禅的随从人员看到蜀国歌舞,想到国家已经灭亡的屈辱,无不伤心落泪,只有刘禅满面春风,嬉笑如常。大家都不能理解。

过了几天,司马昭问起刘禅那天看蜀国歌舞的感受,刘禅对司马昭说:"我在这里很快乐,已经不思念蜀国了。"

司马昭听了刘禅的话,有很多感慨,悄悄对身边的人说:"人之无情,竟然到了这个地步,难怪诸葛亮在世,也救不了蜀国,真是扶不起的阿斗。"

So Happy as to Forget Shu

Paraphrase

Indulge in pleasure, and forget one's home and duty.

Source

Biography of the Later Lord, Book of Shu, Records of the Three Kingdoms: I feel very happy here and don't think about Shu State anymore.

During the Three Kingdoms period, Liu Bei occupied the land of Shu and established Shu State. After Liu Bei's death, his son Liu Shan became the last emperor of Shu State. Liu Shan, nicknamed Adou, did not try to make progress. Even assisted by famous officials like Zhuge Liang, it was of no help. In 263, Shu State was destroyed by Wei State. After Liu Shan **surrendered**, his family was forced to move to Luoyang, the capital of Wei. The King of Wei **conferred** on him the title Duke An Le.

Once, Sima Zhao, a minister of Wei State, hosted a banquet in honor of Liu Shan and deliberately arranging songs and dances of Shu. When Liu Shan's attendants saw the performance of songs and dances of Shu State, thinking of the humiliation of the country's **demise**, they all shed tears, but Liu Shan was smiling and laughing as usual. No one understood him.

surrender
v. 投降

confer
v. 授予

demise
n. 灭亡，终止

A few days later, Sima Zhao asked Liu Shan how he felt about the songs and dances of Shu that day. Liu Shan said to Sima Zhao, "I am very happy here and I don't think of Shu anymore."

After hearing Liu Shan's words, Sima Zhao sighed with emotions. He quietly said to the people around him, "He is so ruthless that it is no wonder Zhuge Liang could not save Shu while he was still alive. Adou is so hopeless."

励精图治

【释义】振奋精神，想办法治理好国家。

【出处】《汉书·魏相传》："宣帝始亲万机，励精为治。"

公元前74年，汉昭帝刘弗陵去世后，因为没有儿子可以继承帝位，当时手握朝政大权的大将军霍光立武帝的曾孙刘询为帝，就是后来的汉宣帝。

公元前68年，霍光病死。御史大夫魏相总结历史教训，考虑到霍氏家族权倾朝野可能带来的危害，建议宣帝采取措施，削弱霍氏家族权力。霍氏家族得知此事后，密谋假借太后之名，先杀魏相，再废宣帝。宣帝得知密报，先发制人，采取行动，族灭霍氏，稳定了政权。

清除了霍氏在朝中的残余势力，汉宣帝得以亲自处理朝政。他振作精神，想方设法，一心要把国家治理得繁荣富强。他民主执政，愿意直接听取大臣的意见，对各级官员严格要求，严格考查，提倡节约，鼓励发展农业生产。魏相带领文武百官，尽职尽责，大家做好分内的事情，很合汉宣帝的心意。

宣帝在魏相的配合下，采取了很多有利于发展生产、减轻人民负担的有效措施，终于使国家兴旺发达起来。宣帝在位25年，让西汉王朝由衰落走向中兴，呈现一派繁荣祥和的景象。

Arouse All Efforts to Make the Country Prosperous

✦ **Paraphrase**

Keep up one's spririts and try to govern the country well.

✦ **Source**

The Biography of Wei Xiang, Book of Han: Emperor Xuan was able to handle the court affairs himself and tried every means to make the country prosperous and strong.

In 74 BC, after the death of Liu Fuling, Emperpor Zhao of Han, the great general Huo Guang, who held the power at the time, appointed Emperor Zhao's great-grandson Liu Xun as the emperor, because Emperor Zhao had no son to inherit the throne. Liu xuan was later known as Emperor Xuan of Han.

In 68 BC, Huo Guang died of illness. Wei Xiang, a senior official, drawing the lessons from history and considering the possible threat caused by Huo family's growing power, suggested that Emperor Xuan take measures to weaken the power of Huo family. After learning of this, Huo family plotted to kill Wei Xiang first and then abolish Emperor Xuan under the **guise** of Queen Mother's order. When Emperor Xuan learned the plot, he

guise
n. 伪装

took action first to destroy Huo family and stabilize the **regime**.

After clearing away Huo's power in the court, Emperor Xuan of the Han Dynasty was able to handle the court affairs himself. He cheered up and tried every means to make the country prosperous and strong. He governed democratically, and was willing to listen to the opinions of those ministers. He was strict with the officials at all levels, and encouraged **thrift** and agricultural development. Wei Xiang led other officials to perform and do their duties well, which was in line with Emperor Xuan's wishes.

With the help of Wei Xiang, Emperor Xuan took many effective measures which were beneficial to the development of production and the ease of the people's burden, and finally made the country prosperous. During his 25 years in power, Emperor Xuan transformed the Western Han Dynasty from decline to **revival**, presenting a prosperous and peaceful scene.

regime
n. 政权

thrift
n. 节俭，节约

revival
n. 振兴，复苏

成语故事

两袖清风

【释义】袖中只有清风,别无所有。比喻做官廉洁。
【出处】《入京》:"清风两袖朝天去,免得闾阎话短长。"

于谦,明朝著名的民族英雄和诗人,出身仕宦世家,从小聪颖过人,承习家教,博览群书,尤其喜读苏武、诸葛亮、岳飞、文天祥等人著述,崇拜他们的正直气节。明宣宗朱瞻基赏识他的学识和品行,破格提拔为河南、山西巡抚。于谦尽管身居高官,依然过着俭朴的生活。

明宣宗去世后,9岁的太子朱祁镇继位,就是明英宗。因为英宗年少,宦官王振专权,以权谋私,每逢朝会,各地官僚为了讨好他,多献以珠宝白银。巡抚于谦从不逢迎他,每次进京奏事,总是不带任何礼品,有人担心于谦因此遭人陷害,就劝说于谦:"你虽然不献金宝、攀求权贵,也可以带些名贵的土特产如线香、蘑菇、手帕等物,送点人情呀!"于谦笑着举起两袖,风趣地说:"我带有两袖清风!"此事过后,于谦写了一首题为《入京》七绝诗:

绢帕蘑菇与线香,本资民用反为殃;

清风两袖朝天去,免得闾阎话短长。

绢帕、蘑菇、线香都是他任职之地的特产。于谦在诗中说,这类东西,本是供人民享用的。只因官吏征调搜刮,反而成了百姓的祸殃了。他在诗中表明自己的态度:我进京什么也不带,只有两袖清风去拜见天子,免得被老百姓看不起,被人耻笑。诗中的"闾阎"是里弄、胡同的意思,引申为民间、老百姓。

Two Sleeves of Breeze

Paraphrase

It literally means nothing but the breeze in the sleeves. It is a metaphor for honest and uncorrupted officials.

Source

Go to the Capital: Go to the capital with two sleeves of breeze to avoid gossip in the alleys.

Yu Qian was a famous national hero and poet in the Ming Dynasty. Born into a family of officials, he had been very intelligent since he was a child. He followed his family's education and read extensively. He especially liked the writings of Su Wu, Zhuge Liang, Yue Fei and Wen Tianxiang, and admired their **integrity**. Zhu Zhanji, Emperor Xuanzong of Ming Dynasty, appreciated his knowledge and conduct and made an exception to promote him to be the governor of Henan and Shanxi. In spite of his high position, Yu Qian still led a simple life.

After the death of Emperor Xuanzong, the 9-year-old prince Zhu Qizhen succeeded to the throne and became Emperor Yingzong. Because Emperor Yingzong was young, the **eunuch** Wang Zhen had the power and used his power for personal gain. Every time at the court meeting, officials from various places often bring some jewels and

integrity

n. 诚实正直

eunuch

n. 宦官

silver to please him. The governor Yu Qian never pleased him. Every time he went to the capital for business, he always brought no gifts. Some people worried that Yu Qian would be framed because of this, so they persuaded Yu Qian, "Although you do not want to give him money or seek power, you may also bring some valuable local products, such as incense, mushrooms, handkerchiefs and so on, so as to offer some favors." Yu Qian raised two sleeves with a smile and said wittily, "I have two sleeves of fresh breeze!" After this, Yu Qian wrote a poem entitled *Go to the Capital* :

Handkerchiefs, mushrooms, and incense, should be for civil use, otherwise, it would bring disasters.

Go to the capital with two sleeves of breeze to avoid gossip in the alleys.

Handkerchief, mushrooms and incense were the local products where he took office. These kinds of things, Yu Qian said in his poem, were originally for common people's use. But due to the levy and plunder from the officials, they became the curse of the people. He expressed his attitude in the poem: I came to the capital with nothing but two sleeves of breeze to visit the emperor, so as not to be looked down upon and laughed at by the common people. Alley in the poem refers to common people.

柳暗花明

【释义】形容柳树成荫、繁花似锦的春天景象。也比喻在困难中遇到转机。

【出处】《游山西村》:"山重水复疑无路,柳暗花明又一村。"

　　南宋爱国诗人陆游,生逢北宋灭亡之际,少年时深受家庭爱国思想的熏陶,一生坚持抗金,屡遭排斥,没有做过高官。老年回到故乡山阴,长期闲居。嘉定二年(1210)去世,留下绝笔《示儿》:"死去元知万事空,但悲不见九州同。王师北定中原日,家祭无忘告乃翁。"表达了他对抗金大业未就的无穷遗恨,也有对神圣事业必成的坚定信念。

　　像陆游这样一位壮志未酬的爱国诗人,闲居在家的滋味一定不好受。陆游闲居的生活就是读书和郊游。他从小就在农村长大,没有当官的架子,和附近的农民混得很熟,成了朋友。

　　这年4月的一天,春光明媚,陆游独自一人到20里外的西山去踏青。登西山要翻过好几个小山头,陆游兴致勃勃,山过了一个又一个,水绕过一道又一道,眼看着已经走到尽头,无路可走,没想到拐过弯来,又是一片山谷幽兰,那里有成荫的绿柳和盛开的红花,沿着溪边还有一个小村庄,村民友善好客,对远道而来的陆游热情招待。

　　回到家后的陆游,久久沉浸在西山之游的兴奋喜悦之中,即兴写了一首七言律诗《游山西村》:

　　莫笑农家腊酒浑,丰年留客足鸡豚。山重水复疑无路,柳暗花明又一村。箫鼓追随春社近,衣冠简朴古风存。从今若许闲乘月,拄杖无时夜叩门。

Beautiful Scene after the Dead End

Paraphrase

It literally means the spring scene with the shade of willow trees and blooming flowers. It is also a metaphor of encountering a turning point in difficulties.

Source

A Trip to West Mountain Village: The mountains **overlap** with twists and turns. I was worried that there would be no way to go. Suddenly, in dense willow trees and bright flowers, a village appeared in front of my eyes.

overlap

v. 重叠

The Southern Song Dynasty patriotic poet Lu You was born at the end of the Northern Song Dynasty. He was deeply influenced by his family's patriotism when he was a boy. He insisted on resisting Jin throughout his life, and was repeatedly rejected. He never served as a high official. In his old age, he returned to his hometown of Shanyin and lived leisurely there for a long time. He died in the second year of Jiading (1210), leaving behind the last poem *To My Son*, "I knew that when I died, everything in the world had nothing to do with me; but the only thing that made me sad was that I didn't see the unity of the motherland with my own eyes. Therefore, the day when the army of the Song Dynasty regained the lost ground in the Central

time. Duke Zhuang was **reluctant** to grant it, but fearing that his mother Jiang would have been very angry at his refusal and did not want to cause discord with his brother, he reluctantly agreed.

reluctant
adj. 不情愿的

Unexpectedly, when Gongshuduan arrived in Jing city, relying on his mother's support, he **recruited** soldiers and bought horses privately, and stored food and fodder, looking for opportunities to seize the throne of his brother's. The behavior of Gongshuduan was already known to everyone, and the ministers went to court, urging Duke Zhuang to make preparations in case of accidents. Duke Zhuang said, "If he does too many bad things, he will surely ruin himself. Just wait and see!"

recruit
v. 征募

Before long, Gongshuduan's power was expanding. He took the opportunity of Duke Zhuang's visit to Luoyang to meet the King of Zhou Dynasty, and captured the capital of Zheng by **collaborating** with his mother, Jiang. It turned out that Duke Zhuang had been prepared for a long time. Not only was it a pretense to see the King of Zhou Dynasty, but he was also planning to drop Gongshuduan's guard. As a matter of fact, Duke Zhuang avoided the attack of the rebels and went out to attack the rebels' **den**. The peasants oppressed by Gongshuduan for a long time supported Duke Zhuang and took part in the battle against the rebels. Duke Zhuang returned to the capital of Zheng with his high-morale army. Defeated and cornered by the chasing soldiers, Gongshuduan committed suicide.

collaborate
v. 合作，协作

den
n. 窝点

Plains, and you hold a family sacrifice, don't forget to tell your father the good news!" It expressed his regret toward the unfinished anti-Jin cause, and the firm belief that the sacred cause would finally succeed.

For a patriotic poet like Lu You with lofty **aspirations**, it must be hard to stay at home idly. What Lu You did in his leisure life was only reading and outings. Growing up in the countryside, he did not have the airs of an official. He became friends with the farmers nearby.

On a beautiful spring day in April of that year, Lu You went for an outing alone in the West Mountain 20 miles away. One needed to climb over several hills before climbing the West Mountain. Feeling very cheerful, Lu You crossed mountains and rivers one after another. When he had come to an dead end and no way out, Lu You didn't expect when he turned around he would see a valley full of shady green willows and blooming red flowers. There was also a small village along the stream, and the villagers were friendly and warmly entertained Lu You from afar.

After returning home, Lu You was immersed in the excitement and joy of his trip to the West Mountain for a long time and wrote an **impromptu** seven-character poem called *A Trip to West Mountain Village* :

Don't laugh at the turbid and muddy wine brewed in the twelfth lunar month, and they entertain guests with rich dishes in the harvest year. The mountains overlap with twists and turns. I was worried that there would be no way to go. Suddenly, in dense willow trees and bright flowers, a village

aspiration

n. 渴望，抱负

impromptu

adj. 即兴的

appeared in front of my eyes. The day of playing the **flute** and the drum in Chunshe(a traditional Chinese festival) is approaching, and the villagers' simple dresses are still preserved. In the future, if I can take a leisure **stroll** in the bright moonlight, I will knock on your door at any time on a walking stick.

flute

n. 长笛，箫

stroll

n. 散步

毛遂自荐

【释义】自己推荐自己。比喻自告奋勇担任某项工作。

【出处】《史记·平原君列传》："今少一人，愿君即以遂备员而行矣。"

公元前 257 年，秦国出兵攻打赵国，包围了赵都邯郸，情况十分危急，赵王派平原君前往楚国求救，希望联楚抗秦。

平原君计划挑选 20 位勇士一同前往，但符合条件的只有 19 位。这时，有个叫毛遂的人，主动向平原君推荐自己，请求加入队伍出征楚国。

平原君问："你来这里已经多久了？"毛遂回答："三年了。"

平原君说："一个真正有才能的人，就好像一把放在袋子里的锥子一样，立刻就会显露出锋利的锥尖。而你来我这里已经三年了，我可从没听说过你，你就不用参加了。"毛遂说："我现在自我推荐，就是请求您把我放进袋子里，看看能不能有施展才华的机会。"

平原君觉得毛遂说得有道理，就答应带他一同前往。

到了楚国，楚王只接见平原君一个人。两人从早晨谈到中午，还没有结果。毛遂大步跨上台阶，远远地大声叫起来："出兵的事，非利即害，非害即利，简单而又明白，为何议而不决？"

楚王非常恼火，大声呵斥："我与平原君说话，谁让你插话？"

毛遂见楚王发怒，不但不退下，反而又走上几个台阶，手按宝剑，毫无惧色地说："大王之所以呵斥我，是仗着在楚国你的地盘。可如今我距大王只有十步之遥，大王您的性命在我手中！"

楚王见毛遂那么勇敢，也心生敬佩，就听毛遂讲述出兵救赵有利楚国的道理，说得楚王心悦诚服，答应马上出兵。毛遂为国家立下了大功，大家对他刮目相看，平原君也待他为上宾。

Mao Sui Recommends Himself

Paraphrase

It means the self-recommendation for a post or task.

Source

Ranked Biographies of Lord Pingyuan, Records of the Grand Historian: Now there is a shortage of one person, and I hope you will let me make up the number to go together.

In 257 BC, Qin State sent troops to attack Zhao and surrounded its capital Handan. The situation was critical. King Zhao sent Lord Pingyuan to Chu State for help, hoping to unite Chu State against Qin State.

Lord Pingyuan planed to select 20 warriors to go together with him, but only 19 were **qualified**. At that time, a person named Mao Sui recommended himself to Lord Pingyuan and asked to join the team to go to Chu State.

Lord Pingyuan asked, "How long have you been here?" Mao Sui replied, "Three years."

Lord Pingyuan said, "A truly talented person is like an awl in a bag, and the sharp point will appear immediately. You have been here for three years, and I have never heard of you. You don't need to join the team." Mao Sui said, "I

qualified

adj. 符合资格的

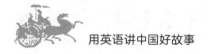

recommend myself now, just to ask you to put me in the bag and see if there is a chance to display my talents."

Lord Pingyuan felt that Mao Sui's words were reasonable, so he promised to take him together.

When they arrived in Chu State, King Chu only **received** Lord Pingyuan. The two talked from morning to noon without any result. Mao Sui then **strode** up the steps and cried out loudly from a distance, "The matter of sending troops is either good or bad, or the other way round. It is simple and clear. Why is it discussed but not decided?"

King Chu was very annoyed and yelled, "I'm talking to Lord Pingyuan. Who allowes you to interrupt?"

When Mao Sui saw that King Chu was angry, he did not retreat. Instead, he went up some steps again, put his hand to his sword, and said without fear, "Your Majesty, the reason why you scolded me is you are in your domain. But now I am only ten steps away from you, and your life is in my hands, Your Majesty!"

Seeing that Mao Sui was so brave, King Chu admired him very much. He listened to Mao Sui's explanation about why Chu should send troops to save Zhao. King Chu was convinced and agreed to send troops immediately. Mao Sui made great contributions to the country. Everyone looked at him with new eyes and Lord Pingyuan treated him as a guest of honor.

receive
v. 接待

stride
v. 大步走

成语故事

名正言顺

【释义】 名义正当,做事、说话有充分理由。
【出处】《论语·子路》:"名不正则言不顺,言不顺则事不利。"

孔子56岁那年,当上了代理宰相,兼管外交事务。这样,孔子有了实现自己政治抱负的机会。他上任才三个月,鲁国风气好转,国力开始增强。齐国的齐景公看在眼里,心中害怕,就设计用美女和骏马诱惑鲁定公,让他沉湎于歌舞淫乐之中,不再过问朝政,听信谗言,排挤孔子。孔子被逼离开自己的国家,开始周游列国。

孔子离开鲁国后,来到了卫国。卫灵公问孔子在鲁国的俸禄是多少,孔子说是俸米六万斗。于是卫灵公也给他这个数量的俸米。孔子的学生子路问孔子:"如果卫灵公需要你去帮助治理国政,你准备首先做什么呢?"

孔子说:"我以为首先要纠正名分。"

子路不解地说:"老师未免太迂腐了,这有纠正的必要吗?"

孔子说:"你真是幼稚啊!名分不正,道理也就讲不通;道理不通,事情也就办不成;事情办不成,国家的礼乐教化也就兴办不起来;礼乐教化兴办不起来,刑罚就不会得当;刑罚不得当,老百姓就会没有是非之分,连手脚都不晓得往何处放了。所以君子用的名分,一定要有道理可以说得出来,讲出来的道理也一定要行得通。"

不久,卫灵公听信谗言,不再信任孔子,还派人监视孔子的行动。孔子感到继续留在卫国已经没有意义,在卫国居住十个月后,就无奈地离开了。

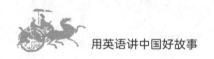

Right Titles and Proper Words

Paraphrase

It means the name is legitimate, and there are good reasons for acting and speaking.

Source

Zilu in The Analects: If the title is not justified, the words can not be reasonalbe; if the words is not reasonable, things can not be done.

When Confucius was 56 years old, he became acting prime minister and was in charge of foreign affairs. In this way, Confucius had the opportunity to realize his political ambitions. When he had been in office for only three months, the morale of Lu State had improved and the national strength has begun to increase. Seeing this, Duke Jing of Qi began to be fearful. He plotted to corrupt Duke Ding of Lu State with beauties and steeds so that Duke Ding would indulge in singing, dancing and music, and was no longer concerned about government affairs. Hearing and believing **slanders**, Duke Ding excluded Confucius. Confucius was forced to leave his country and began to travel around the states.

After Confucius left Lu State, he came to Wei State. Duke Ling of Wei asked Confucius what his salary in Lu

slander

n. 口头诽谤

was, and Confucius said it was 60,000 *dou* of rice. So Duke Ling gave him the same pay. Confucius' student Zilu asked Confucius, "If Duke Ling needs you to help him govern the state, what are you going to do first?"

Confucius said, "I think the first thing is to justify my title."

Zilu said in a puzzled way: "My teacher, you are too **pedantic**. Is there a need for this?"

Confucius said, "You are so naive! If your title is not justified, the truth can not be passed; if the truth is not passed, things can not be done; if things cannot be done, the education of rites and music of the country cannot be started; if the education of rites and music cannot be carried out, the punishment will not be proper; if the punishment is not proper, the people will not tell right from wrong, and they don't even know where to put their hands and feet. Therefore, the title of a gentleman must be justifiable and the truth told must make sense."

Before long, Duke Ling of Wei believed slanders and did not trust Confucius any more. He also sent people to monitor Confucius. Confucius felt that there was no point to stay in Wei. After ten months of living there, he had no choice but to leave.

pedantic

adj. 迂腐的

磨杵成针

【释义】把铁棒磨成了针。比喻做任何艰难的工作,只要有毅力,下苦功,就能够克服困难,做出成绩。

【出处】《潜确类书》:"道逢老妪磨杵,白问其故。曰:'欲作针。'"

四川省眉山一带,有一条小溪,叫磨针溪,相传与唐代大诗人李白有关。

李白小时候非常贪玩,不肯好好学习。有一天,他趁老师不注意,偷偷溜了出去闲逛,不知不觉来到了一条小溪旁边,看见一个老婆婆正在一块石头上磨着一根铁棒子。

李白很奇怪,上前问道:"老婆婆,您为什么要磨这根铁棒子呢?"

老婆婆回答说:"我要把这根铁棒磨成一根绣花针!"

李白听了老婆婆的话更惊讶了。这么粗的铁棒,要磨到什么时候才能磨成针呢?老婆婆见李白有些疑惑,就向他解释说:"只要功夫深,铁棒也能磨成绣花针!"

李白听了老婆婆的话,很受震动。他想一个白发苍苍的老婆婆还满怀信心地要把铁棒磨成绣花针,我年纪轻轻的为什么不能克服困难好好地学习呢?于是他马上回去向老师道歉,保证今后一定会努力读书。

据说那老妇人自称姓武,现在磨针溪边还有一块武氏岩。

Grind an Iron Bar down to a Needle

❖ Paraphrase

Grind the iron bar into a needle. It means as long as you have perseverance and work hard, you can overcome difficulties and make achievements in doing any difficult job.

❖ Source

A Reference Book by Qian Que: He saw an old woman grinding an iron bar on a stone and asked why. The old woman replied, "I want to grind this iron bar into a needle!"

In Mount Mei area of Sichuan Province, there is a stream called Mozhen (grinding the needle) Stream, which is said to be related to the great poet Li Bai of the Tang Dynasty.

Li Bai was very playful when he was young and refused to study hard. One day, when the teacher wasn't paying attention to him, he slipped out and wandered around. He came to a stream and saw an old woman grinding an iron bar on a stone.

Li Bai was very curious and asked, "Grandma, why are you grinding this iron bar?"

The old woman replied, "I want to grind this iron bar

into an **embroidery** needle!"

Li Bai was even more surprised at the old woman's words. How long would it take to grind such a thick iron bar into a needle? Seeing Li Bai's doubt, the old woman explained to him, "If you work hard enough, even an iron bar can be ground into a needle!"

Li Bai was moved by what the old woman said. He thought that a gray-haired old woman was confident that she would grind the iron bar into a needle, so why couldn't he overcome the difficulties and study hard at a young age? So he immediately went back to **apologize** to the teacher and promised to study hard in the future.

It is said that the old woman called herself Wu, and now there is still a stone called Wu Rock beside Mozhen Stream.

embroidery

n. 绣花

apologize

v. 道歉

成语故事

南辕北辙

【释义】心想往南而车子却向北行。比喻行动和目的正好相反。

【出处】《战国策·魏策四》:"犹至楚而北行也。"

战国末期,魏国日渐衰弱,但魏王仍然想攻打赵国,扩大自己的影响力。正在出访的大臣季梁听说后,马上中止外访活动,赶回国内,劝说魏王放弃攻打赵国的念头。他知道如果直接提出反对意见,魏王肯定听不进去,就想了个办法。

季梁对魏王说:"我今天回来时,在路遇见一个人,他要到楚国去却坐车往北走。我问他,楚国在南面,你怎么往北走呢?那人说,没关系,他的马跑得快。我说你马跑得快也没用,往北不是楚国的方向。那人说,没关系,我有足够去楚国路费。我说你路费再多也没用,方向反了,永远也到不了楚国。那人说,没关系,我的马夫最会赶车了。这人真的是无法理解,马跑得越快,路费带得越多、马夫越会赶车,离楚国的距离越远。"

魏王说:"这人是真的糊涂,方向不对,条件越好,离目标越远。"

听魏王这么说,季梁马上说到正题:"大王啊,如今您想成就伟业,一举一动都要取信于天下,方能树立权威。如果依仗武力征服他人,必定不能收复人心,就像那个坐车往北走的人,只会事与愿违,达不到想要的目标。"

魏王听后,为季梁的忠心和用心所感动,决定取消进攻赵国的计划。

Go South by Driving Northward

Paraphrase

I want to go south but the carriage goes north. It is a metaphor that action and purpose are just the opposite.

Source

Strategies of Wei IV, Strategies of the Warring States: Just like someone who wants to go to Chu by driving northward.

At the end of the Warring States Period, Wei State became weaker and weaker. However, King Wei still wanted to attack Zhao and expand his influence. When Ji Liang heard of this, he immediately stopped his foreign visit and returned home to persuade King Wei to give up the idea of attacking Zhao State. He knew that King Wei would not listen to any direct objection, so he came up with an idea.

Ji Liang said to King Wei, "When I came back today, I met a man on the road who was driving north to Chu State. I told him that Chu State was in the south. How would he go north? The man said that was okay and his horse ran fast. I said it was useless for his horse to run fast. North was not the direction of Chu State. The man said that was okay and he had enough travel expenses to

go to Chu State. I said it didn't help no matter how much money he had when the direction was wrong, and he would never reach Chu State. The man said, that was okay and his horseman was best at riding. The man just couldn't understand that the faster the horse runs, the more money he will have to pay for the journey and the more capable the horseman is, the farther he will be from Chu State."

King Wei said, "This man is really confused. He is in the wrong direction. The better the conditions are, the farther away he is from his target."

When King Wei said this, Ji Liang immediately came to the point, "Your Majesty, now you want to achieve a great cause. You must win the trust of the world in every move so that you can establish your authority. If you conquer others by force, you cannot win people's hearts, just like the man who drives to the north can only achieve the opposite of what he wants."

After hearing this, King Wei was moved by Ji Liang's loyalty and dedication and decided to cancel the plan to attack Zhao State.

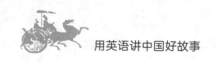

呕心沥血

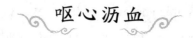

【释义】比喻费尽心血。
【出处】《归彭城》："刳肝以为纸，沥血以书辞。"

唐朝著名诗人李贺，从小就很聪明，七岁就开始写诗做文，才华横溢。大诗人韩愈开始不相信，曾现场出题让他写诗，李贺不假思索，提笔成诗，由此出名。

李贺有一个习惯，写诗不搞主题先行，而是到生活中去发掘题材。他每次外出，都让书童背一个袋子，只要一有灵感，想出几句好诗，就马上记下来，放到袋子里，回家后再重新整理成诗。

李贺身体单薄，一心都在写诗上，母亲非常担心，心疼地说："这孩子是把全部的精力放在写诗上了，真是要把心呕出来才罢休啊！"李贺在他短暂的27年生涯中，留下了240余首诗歌，这是他用毕生的心血凝成的。

唐代文学家韩愈曾写过这样两句诗："刳肝以为纸，沥血以书辞。"即是说挖出心肝来当纸，滴出血来写文章。后人遂把两者合称为"呕心沥血"。

Spit out the Heart and Spill the Blood

❋ **Paraphrase**

It is a metaphor of **exerting** one's utmost effort.

❋ **Source**

Return to Peng: Cut liver as paper, and drip blood to write.

exert
v. 运用，行使

Li He, a famous poet in the Tang Dynasty, was very smart from an early age. He began to write poetry and essays at the age of seven, and was extremely talented. The great poet Han Yu didn't believe it at first, and he once asked Li He to write a poem on the spot. Li He picked up the brush and wrote a poem without thinking, and thus became famous.

Li He had a habit of discovering themes in daily life instead of thinking of a theme before writing a poem. Every time he went out, he asked a boy, his servant, to carry a bag. As long as he had inspiration and came up with good lines, he immediately wrote them down, put them in the bag, and reorganized them into poems when he returned home.

Li He was weak and devoted himself to writing poetry. His mother was very worried and said lovingly, "The child has devoted all his energy to writing poetry. He will only stop until he works his heart out!" In his short 27-year life, Li He left more than 240 poems, which he had dedicated his life to.

Han Yu, a writer in the Tang Dynasty, once wrote two lines of poems: "Cut liver as paper, and drip blood to write." That is to say, dig out the heart and liver to be used as papers and drip blood to write an article. Later generations called the two lines together as "spit out the heart and **spill** the blood".

spill

v. 洒出

披荆斩棘

【释义】劈开丛生多刺的野生植物。比喻在创业过程中或前进道路上清除障碍，克服重重困难。

【出处】《后汉书·冯异传》："为吾披荆棘，定关中。"

冯异是东汉光武帝刘秀手下的一员大将，多次随刘秀出征，取得赫赫战功，却淡漠名利，从不邀功请赏。

刘秀在洛阳建立东汉政权后，任命冯异为征西大将军，平定关中起义军以后，长期镇守长安，称为咸阳王。有人嫉妒冯异的权势，就向刘秀告冯异的黑状，说冯异权力过大，如果不加控制，迟早会谋反。冯异得知消息后，马上给刘秀上奏，表明自己的忠心，说："过去那么艰苦的条件，我都坚定不移地追随皇上，现在天下太平，皇帝又给了我重要的职位，我怎么会谋反呢？我效忠您的心从来没有变过。"

刘秀对冯异的为人品行非常清楚，就在回信中说："我和将军虽然是君臣，但私底下亲如父子。我对将军从来没有怀疑过，你又何必担惊受怕呢？"

后来，冯异从长安回到洛阳拜见刘秀，刘秀当着朝廷文武百官的面，拉着冯异的手说："这是我起兵时的主簿，为我披荆斩棘，平定了关中。"此后再也没人在光武帝面前说冯异的坏话了。

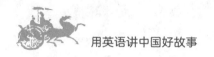

Break Open a Way Through Thistles and Thorns

Paraphrase

Split the bushy and thorny wild plants. It is a metaphor of clearing obstacles and overcoming difficulties in the process of starting a business or on the road ahead.

Source

The Biography of Feng Yi, History of Later Han Dynasty: He broke open a way through thistles and thorns for me, and **pacified** Guanzhong.

pacify
v. 平定

Feng Yi was a general under Liu Xiu, Emperor Guangwu of the Eastern Han Dynasty. He went to war with Liu Xiu for many times and made great military achievements. However, he cared little about fame and wealth and never asked for credit or rewards.

After Liu Xiu established the regime of the Eastern Han Dynasty in Luoyang, he appointed Feng Yi as the General West March. After he put down the rebellion in Guanzhong, he defended Chang'an for a long time and was called King Xianyang. Someone was jealous of Feng Yi's power and brought some false **charge** to Liu Xiong against Feng Yi, saying that Feng Yi got too much power and would rebel sooner or later if his power was out of

charge
n. 控告

control. When Feng Yi heard the news, he wrote to Liu Xiu immediately, expressing his loyalty, saying, "In the past, under such difficult conditions, I **unswervingly** followed Your Majesty. Now the country is peaceful and Your Majesty has given me an important position. How can I rebel? My loyalty to you has never changed."

Liu Xiu was very clear about Feng Yi's morality, and wrote back, "Although the general and I are monarch and minister, we are like father and son in private. I have never doubted you. Why should you be scared?"

Later, Feng Yi went from Chang'an to Luoyang to see Liu Xiu. Liu Xiu took Feng Yi's hands and said in front of the officials, "This is my chief secretary when I started wars. He broke open a way through thistles and thorns for me, and pacified Guanzhong." Since then, no one said anything bad about Feng Yi in front of Emperor Guangwu.

unswervingly

adv. 坚定不移地

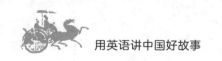

破釜沉舟

【释义】把饭锅打破，把渡船凿沉；表示下定决心，为取得胜利可以牺牲一切。

【出处】《史记·项羽本纪》："项羽乃悉引兵渡河，皆沉船，破釜甑，烧庐舍，持三日粮，以示士卒必死，无一还心。"

秦朝末年，秦军攻打赵国，赵王从都城邯郸退守到巨鹿，被秦军团团围住。赵王派人向楚国求救。楚怀王派宋义为上将军，项羽为次将，带领20万军队前去救赵国。

宋义率军驻扎安阳后，46天按兵不动。项羽催促宋义说："秦军包围了巨鹿，形势紧急，我军赶快过河，与赵军里外夹击，打败秦军。"

宋义坚持等到秦军和赵军两败俱伤后，再发起进攻。他对项羽说："上阵打仗，我比不上你；但说到运筹帷幄，出谋划策，你比不上我。"还下了一道命令："有不服从者，军法处死！"

当时已经入冬，天寒地冻，士兵挨冻受饿，抱怨的情绪日益高涨。项羽利用这种情绪，鼓动士兵，找机会把宋义杀了。项羽为上将军，亲自率军过河，赶往巨鹿，以解被困之围。

楚军全部渡河以后，项羽让士兵们饱饱地吃了一顿饭，每人再带三天干粮，然后传下命令："把渡河的船凿穿沉入河里，把做饭用的锅砸个粉碎，把附近的房屋放把火统统烧毁。"项羽用这种破釜沉舟的办法，表达他有进无退、夺取胜利的决心。

没有退路的楚军以一当十，经过九次激战，最终大破秦军，不仅解了巨鹿之围，而且给秦军致命一击。两年后，秦朝灭亡。

Break the Pots and Sink the Boats

Paraphrase

Break the pots and sink the boats, which is used to express one's determination to sacrifice everything for victory.

Source

Basic Annals of Xiang Yu, Records of the Grand Historian: Xiang Yu led the troops to cross the river, and then ask the soldiers to sink the boats, break the pots, burn the houses, and bring food for three days to show his determination to go forward without retreat.

In the last years of the Qin Dynasty, the Qin army attacked Zhao State, and King Zhao retreated from the capital Handan to Julu, and was surrounded by the Qin army. King Zhao sent someone to ask for help from Chu State. King Huai of Chu sent Song Yi as the general and Xiang Yu as the second general, leading an army of 200,000 to rescue Zhao State.

After Song Yi led his army to Anyang, he stayed there for 46 days. Xiang Yu urged Song Yi, "The Qin army has surrounded Julu. The situation is **urgent**. Our army should quickly cross the river and fight with Zhao army to defeat Qin army."

urgent

adj. 紧急的，紧迫的

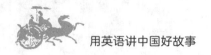

Song Yi insisted on waiting until Qin army and Zhao army were both injured before launching an attack. He said to Xiang Yu, "In terms of battle, I am no match for you; but when it comes to strategizing and making suggestions, you are no match for me." He also issued an order, "Those who disobey will be **executed** by military law!"

It was winter, and the soldiers were cold, hungry, and their complaints were growing. Xiang Yu took advantage of this emotion and encouraged the soldiers to kill Song Yi. When Xiang Yu became the general, he led his troops across the river to Julu to relieve Zhao State from the siege.

After all Chu army had crossed the river, Xiang Yu let the soldiers have a full meal, and each of them brought food for three days. Then he gave the orders, "Sink the boats into the river, smash the cooking pots into pieces, and set all the houses nearby on fire." In this way, Xiang Yu showed his determination to go forward without retreat.

After nine fierce battles, Chu army, which had no way of retreat, finally broke through Qin army, not only breaking the siege of Julu, but also giving Qin army a fatal blow. Two years later, the Qin Dynasty fell.

execute
v.（尤指依法）处决，处死

七步之才

【释义】在七步之内,写成一首诗。形容才思敏捷。

【出处】《世说新语·文学》:"文帝尝令东阿王七步中作诗,不成者行大法。"

曹植是三国时期著名诗人、文学家。他是曹操的儿子,魏文帝曹丕的同母弟弟。曹植从小受到良好的文学熏陶,有非凡的文学才华,深受父王曹操宠爱,曹操几次想要立他为世子,继承大业,终因为曹植生性随意,让曹操犹豫未决。

曹丕一心想当魏世子,平时处处小心博得父王好感,在一些人的保荐下,公元217年被立为世子。三年后,曹操病逝,曹丕即位,废汉献帝,自立为帝,即魏文帝。

曹丕称帝后,对曹植仍不放心,借口曹植在父丧期间礼仪不当,将其拿下问罪,罪当处死。审讯的时候,曹丕指责他仗着自己的才学,故意蔑视礼法,说:"父王在世时,常夸你的诗文,我一直怀疑有人为你代笔。今天限你七步成诗一首,如若不成,休怪我问你死罪!"曹植点头,说:"请皇上赐题。"曹丕想了想,说:"就以兄弟为题,但不许出现兄弟二字。"

曹植略一思忖,便迈开脚步,走一步吟一句:"煮豆持作羹,漉菽以为汁。萁在釜下燃,豆在釜中泣。本自同根生,相煎何太急?"这几句诗的意思是:要煮豆子作豆豉,抱来豆梗当柴烧。豆梗在锅下燃烧,豆子在锅里哭泣。你我本来是一条根上长出来的,为什么要这样狠心地煮我呢?曹植吟完,正好走了七步。曹丕听了,羞愧难当,免去了他的死罪,将他贬为安乡侯。曹植七步成诗的事很快传开,人们也因此而称赞他有"七步之才"。

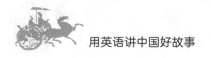

Seven-step Talent

Paraphrase

Write a poem in seven steps. It refers to people's quick mind.

Source

Literature, A New Account of the Tales of the World: Emperor Wen of Wei once ordered the East King Cao Zhi to compose a poem within seven steps and would be sentenced to death if he failed to do so.

Cao Zhi was a famous poet and writer in the Three Kingdoms period. He was the son of Cao Cao and younger brother of Cao Pi, Emperor Wen of Wei, who had the same mother. He was influenced by good literature since he was a child and possessed extraordinary literary talent. He was deeply loved by his father Cao Cao. Cao Cao wanted to make him the crown prince to inherit his great cause several times. However, Cao Cao hesitated because of Cao Zhi's casual nature.

Cao Pi wanted to be the crown prince, and he was always careful to win the favor of his father. With the **sponsors** of some people, he became the crown prince in 217. Three years later, Cao Cao died of illness, and Cao Pi **ascended** to the throne. He **deposed** Emperor Xian of the

sponsor
n. 保证人
ascend
v. 登基
depose
v. 罢免，废黜

Han Dynasty and made himself as Emperor Wen of Wei.

After Cao Pi became the emperor, he was still worried about Cao Zhi. He arrested Cao Zhi and sentenced him to death with an excuse of his improper **etiquette** during his father's funeral. During the **interrogation**, Cao Pi accused him of deliberately **flouting propriety** by relying on his talents, "When our father was alive, he often praised your poems. I always doubt that there is someone writing for you. Today you must write a poem within seven steps. If you failed, don't blame me for sentencing you to death!" Cao Zhi nodded and said, "Please assign a topic, Your Majesty." Cao Pi thought for a while and said, "Just use 'brother' as the topic, but the word 'brother' is not allowed to appear in the poem."

Cao Zhi thought for a while, then stepped forward, and said, "Boil the beans to make soup. Filter the residue and keep the juice. The stalks are burning under the pot, and the beans are weeping in the pot. Grown from the same root, why are they so urgent to boil each other?" The meaning of this poems is: "Boil beans to make the bean paste, and hold bean stalks as firewood. The bean stalks burned under the pot, and the beans cried in the pot. You and I grew out of one root, so why did you boil me so cruelly?" Cao Zhi finished his poem and took exactly seven steps. Cao Pi was ashamed. He spared his death penalty and relegated him as Duke An Xiang. The story that Cao Zhi wrote a poem within seven steps was quickly spread around, and people praised him for his "seven-step talent".

etiquette
n. 礼节，礼仪

interrogation
n. 讯问，审问

flout
v. 公然蔑视，无视（法律等）

propriety
n. 行为规范，规矩

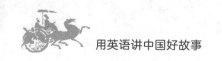

杞人忧天

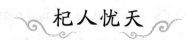

【释义】比喻没必要的担心或者不切实际的忧虑。

【出处】《列子·天瑞》:"杞国有人,忧天地崩坠,身亡所寄,废寝食者。"

从前,杞国有个人,整天担心天会塌下来,地会陷下去,到那个时候,自己和所有人都将无处依托。为此,他吃不好饭,睡不着觉。

有人见此情形,就去开导他,说:"天不过是积聚的气体罢了,没有哪个地方没有空气的。你一举一动,一呼一吸,都在天空里活动,怎么还担心天会塌下来呢?"

那人说:"天是气体,那日、月、星、辰不就会掉下来吗?"

开导他的人说:"日、月、星、辰也是空气中发光的东西,即使掉下来,也不会有什么伤害。"

那人又说:"如果地陷下去怎么办?"

开导他的人说:"地不过是堆积的土块罢了,填满了四处,没有什么地方是没有土块的,你行走跳跃,都在地上活动,怎么还担心地会陷下去呢?"

听了这个人的解释,那个杞国人才放下心来。

成语故事

The Man of Qi State Worried That the Sky Would Fall

✤ **Paraphrase**

It means unnecessary or unrealistic worry.

✤ **Source**

Heaven's Gifts, Liezi: There is a man of Qi State who worried that the sky would fall down and the earth would cave in so that people had nowhere to stay, and thus he could not eat nor sleep well.

Once upon a time, there was a man of Qi State who worried all day long that the sky would fall down and the earth would cave in. At that time, he and everyone else would have nowhere to stay. For this reason, he could not eat well nor sleep well.

Someone saw this and went to enlighten him, saying, "The day is only the **accumulation** of gas, and there is no place without air. Every move you make, every breath you take, you do it in the sky. How can you worry that the sky will fall down?"

The man said, "The sky is gas, but won't the sun, moon, and stars fall?"

The person who enlightened him said, "The sun, the moon, and the stars are some **luminous** things in the air.

accumulation

n. 聚合物

luminous

adj. 发光的

143

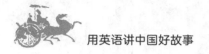

Even if they fall, there will be no harm."

The man said again, "What if the ground sinks?"

The person who enlightened him said: "The ground is nothing more than a pile of **clods**. It fills up everywhere. There is no place without clods. You walk and jump, all on the ground. Why are you worried that the ground will sink?"

After listening to this person's explanation, the man of Qi State was finally relieved.

clod
n. 泥块，土块

成语故事

千里之堤，毁于蚁穴

【释义】一个小小的蚂蚁洞，可以使千里长堤毁于一旦。比喻小事不注意会造成大乱子。

【出处】《韩非子·喻老》："千丈之堤，以蝼蚁之穴溃；百尺之室，以突隙之烟焚。"

有一年，黄河岸边有一片村庄，为了防止洪水泛滥成灾，造成村民生命和财产损失，村民们在黄河和村庄之间，筑起了一条长长的防洪堤。

有个老农下地种田，偶然发现堤坝多处出现了蚂蚁窝。老农马上想到，这些蚂蚁窝会不会影响堤坝的安全。他决定赶回村里汇报情况。

回村的路上，老农遇见了他儿子。儿子见父亲这么急匆匆地赶路，就问怎么回事。老农把多处发现蚂蚁窝的事对儿子说了。儿子听了不以为然，对父亲说："您老人家真是多虑了。这么坚固的堤坝，小小的蚂蚁怎么会有影响呢？"

老农想想觉得也有道理，就和儿子一起下地种田了。

此后一连几日，大雨不停，山洪暴发，河水猛涨。洪水从蚂蚁窝渗透出来，继而形成管涌，从大堤多个蚂蚁窝里喷出来，造成无法挽回的后果。

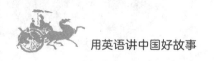

用英语讲中国好故事

A Thousand-mile Long Dam Can Be Destroyed by Ant Nests

Paraphrase

A small ant nest can destroy a great dam of thousands of miles. It means paying no attention to little harmful things can cause great trouble.

Source

Illustrations of Lao Tzu's Teachings, Han Feizi: A thousand-mile dam could be destroyed by ant nests; a hundred-foot tall building may be burned down by sparks from the gaps in the chimney.

There was a village on the bank of the Yellow River. One year, in order to prevent the floods from causing damage to the lives and property of the villagers, the villagers built a long dam between the Yellow River and the village.

An old farmer went to the fields and happened to find many ant nests on the dam. The old farmer immediately worried that these ant nests would affect the safety of the dam. He decided to rush back to the village to report the situation.

On the way back to the village, the old farmer met his son. Seeing that his father was in such a hurry, the son

asked what was the matter. The old farmer told his son about the discovery of ant nests. After hearing this, the son disapproved, and said to his father, "You are really worrying too much. How can little ants have any effect on such a strong dam?"

The old farmer thought about it and found it reasonable, so he went to farm with his son.

For several days thereafter, heavy rains fell and lasted for days, flash floods broke out, and river water surged. The flood water **seeped** out from the ant nests, and then caused piping effect, **spewed** out from multiple ant nests on the dam, causing **irreversible** consequences.

seep
v. 渗，渗透
spew
v. 喷出，涌出
irreversible
adj. 无法复原的

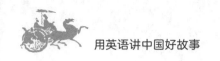

前事不忘后事之师

【释义】比喻人们应当牢记以前的经验教训，作为今后行事的借鉴。
【出处】《战国策·赵策一》："前事之不忘，后事之师。"

春秋末年，晋国的大权落到智伯、赵襄子、魏桓子、韩康子四位大臣手中。

公元前458年（已进入战国时期），晋定公病死，智伯独揽朝政大权。他以增强晋国实力为由，建议四位大臣各拿出一百里土地和一个万户规模的城市，奉献给国家。智伯自己带头奉献，魏桓子、韩康子迫于智伯的权威，也照办了，只有赵襄子严词拒绝，揭露智伯是以此为借口削弱他人势力。智伯立即派人传令，让魏桓子和韩康子一起去攻打赵襄子。

智伯率魏、韩两家攻打晋阳。晋阳被智伯围困了整整三年，形势越来越危急。一天，张孟谈面见赵襄子，说："魏、韩两家攻打我们，完全是被迫的。我去向他们说明利害，动员他们反戈联赵，共同消灭智伯。"

当天夜晚，张孟谈潜入魏、韩营中，说服了魏桓子和韩康子。赵、魏、韩三家联合进攻，智伯被擒。从此，晋国成了赵、魏、韩三家鼎立的局面。

张孟谈向赵襄子告别，赵襄子急忙挽留。张孟谈说："您想的是报答我的功劳，我想的是治国的道理。正因为我的功劳大，在外的名声可能超过您，所以才决心离开。历史上从来没有君臣权势相同而永远和好相处的。'前事不忘，后事之师。'请您让我走吧！"

赵襄子只好惋惜地答应了。张孟谈辞去官职，退还封地，隐居乡野，平安地度过了自己的晚年。

The Past Is the Teacher of the Future

❖ Paraphrase

It is a metaphor that people should keep in mind the previous experience and lessons as a reference for future actions.

❖ Source

Strategies of Zhao I, Strategies of the Warring States: Lessons learned from the past can guide one in the future.

At the end of the Spring and Autumn Period, the power of Jin State fell to the four ministers, Zhi Bo, Zhao Xiangzi, Wei Huanzi, and Han Kangzi.

In 458 BC(during the Warring States Period), Duke Ding of Jin died of illness, and Zhi Bo took the power of the court. On the pretext of strengthening Jin State, he suggested that each of the four ministers devote one hundred *li* of land and a city of ten thousand households to the state. Zhi Bo took the lead in dedication, and Wei Huanzi and Han Kangzi were forced by the authority of Zhi Bo and followed suit. Only Zhao Xiangzi **sternly** refused, exposing Zhi Bo's excuse to weaken the power of the others. Zhi Bo immediately sent someone to pass the order, letting Wei Huanzi and Han Kangzi attack Zhao Xiangzi together.

sternly
adv. 严厉

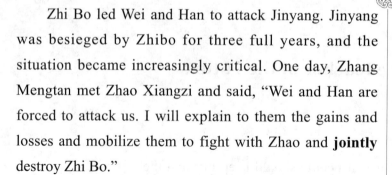

Zhi Bo led Wei and Han to attack Jinyang. Jinyang was besieged by Zhibo for three full years, and the situation became increasingly critical. One day, Zhang Mengtan met Zhao Xiangzi and said, "Wei and Han are forced to attack us. I will explain to them the gains and losses and mobilize them to fight with Zhao and **jointly** destroy Zhi Bo."

jointly
adv. 共同地

That night, Zhang Mengtan sneaked into the camp of Wei and Han and persuaded Wei Huanzi, and Han Kangzi. Zhao, Wei and Han joint forces and attacked Zhi Bo together, and Zhi Bo was captured. Since then, Jin had come to a situation where Zhao, Wei and Han stood together.

Zhang Mengtan **bid** farewell to Zhao Xiangzi, who hurriedly ask Zhang Mengtan to stay. Zhang said, "What you are thinking about is repaying my contributions. What I am thinking about is the principle of governing the country. I have done so much that I may be better known outside than you, so I am determined to leave. There has never been a monarch and minister with the same power and can always get along well. 'The past is the teacher of the future.' Please let me go!"

bid
v. 表示

Zhao Xiangzi had to agree regretfully. Zhang Mengtan resigned his post, returned his **fief**, retired to the countryside, and spent his old age in peace.

fief
n. 领地

黔驴技穷

【释义】有限的本领已经用尽。

【出处】《三戒·黔之驴》:"驴不胜怒,蹄之。虎因喜,计之曰:'技止此耳!'"

古时候,贵州一带没有驴,人们对驴的相貌、习性、用途等都不了解。有个喜欢多事的人,从外地用船运来了一头驴,可是一时又不知该怎么用,就把它放养在山脚下。

山上有一只老虎,从来没有见过驴。第一次看到这家伙身躯庞大,以为是神兽,非常害怕,不敢靠近,只躲在密密的树林里,偷偷观察。

有一天,老虎小心翼翼地接近它。驴忽然长叫了一声,声音很大,吓得老虎拔腿就跑,跑到远处,发现那个庞然大物并没有追上来,就坐下来仔仔细细地观察,猜想它有什么特别厉害的本领。

又过了几天,老虎习惯了驴的叫声,胆子更大,敢走到驴身边,围着它又叫又跳,有时还跑过去故意冒犯它,又马上跑开。

终于,驴被老虎戏弄得发怒了,它抬起蹄子猛踢过去,老虎慌忙躲开。开始的时候,老虎还有些惊惶,几次试探过后,发现驴就只有这么一点伎俩,就嘲笑驴说:"你这个没用的大家伙,原来也就这么点本事啊!"说着,扑上去,把驴吃了。

The Donkey of Qian Exhausted Its Tricks

✦ **Paraphrase**

The limited ability has been exhausted.

✦ **Source**

The Donkey of Qian, Three Commandments: The donkey was **irritated** and raised its **hoof** to kick. The tiger laughed, " That's all you've got!"

irritate

v. 使烦恼

hoof

n. 蹄

In ancient times, there were no donkeys in Guizhou, so people did not know about their appearance, habits or uses. A man who liked looking for trouble brought a donkey by boat from other places, but he didn't know how to use it, so he put it at the foot of the mountain.

There was a tiger on the mountain. He had never seen a donkey before. The first time he saw this huge animal, he thought it was a **mythical** creature. He was so afraid that he dared not come near it. The tiger only hid in the dense woods and observed it secretly.

mythical

adj. 神话里的

One day, the tiger approached it cautiously. The donkey suddenly gave a loud cry. The tiger was scared and ran away. He found that the huge monster didn't catch up with him, so he sat down and observed it carefully to see what other special skills it had.

After a few days, the tiger got used to the donkey's

cry and became braver. He dared to walk to the donkey, **roaring** and jumping around it. Sometimes, he even ran to **offend** the donkey deliberately and ran away immediately.

Finally, the donkey was irritated by the tiger's **teasing**. It raised its hoof and kicked the tiger, and the tiger hurriedly avoided it. At the beginning, the tiger was a little frightened. After several trials, he found that the donkey had only such a trick. He laughed at the donkey and said, "You are a useless big guy. That's all you've got!" With that he jumped on the donkey and ate it.

roar
v. 吼叫

offend
v. 冒犯

tease
v. 取笑，戏弄

穷兵黩武

【释义】 随意使用武力，不断发动侵略战争。形容极其好战。

【出处】《三国志·吴书·陆抗传》："穷兵黩武，动费万计。"

三国时期，东吴后期的名将陆抗，是陆逊的儿子，孙策的外孙。公元264年，孙皓当了东吴的国君，38岁的陆抗担任镇军大将军。

当时，东吴的朝政非常腐败。孙皓是个暴君，生活荒淫无度，对外耀武扬威，军队人数达到百姓人数的十分之一，军费开支大，国库空虚，民不聊生。

陆抗对孙皓的所作所为非常不满，多次上疏，劝谏他对外加强防守，对内改善政治，以增强国力。他曾在奏疏中一次陈述当前应做的事达16件之多。孙皓都置之不理。

公元272年，吴将步阐投降晋国，陆抗率军征讨，击退来援的晋军，杀死叛将步阐，逼迫晋国与东吴议和，边境地带一时出现了和好的局面。孙皓对此很不高兴，派人责问陆抗，仍然想出兵攻晋。

陆抗见军队不断出动，百姓精疲力竭，便向孙皓上疏说："现在朝廷不从事富国强兵，加紧农业生产，储备粮食，让有才能的人发挥作用，使各级官署不荒怠职守，严明升迁制度以激励百官，审慎实施刑罚以警戒百姓，用道德教导官吏，以仁义安抚百姓，反而听任众将追求名声，用尽所有兵力，好战不止，耗费的资财动以万计，士兵疲劳不堪。这样，敌人没有削弱，而我们自己倒像生了一场大病。"

陆抗还郑重指出："吴、晋两国实力不同，今天即使出兵获胜，也得不偿失。所以，应该停止用兵，积蓄力量，以待时机。"但是，孙皓对陆抗的这些忠告都听不进去。后来陆抗去世，晋军讨伐东吴，沿着长江顺流东下，势如破竹，吴国终于被晋国所灭。

成语故事

Exhaust the Troops and Engage in Wars

❋ Paraphrase

Use force at will and continuously **launch** wars of aggression. It refers to people who are extremely aggressive.

❋ Source

The Biography of Lu Kang, Book of Wu, Records of Three Kingdoms: Exhaust the troops and engage in wars at a cost of a lot of money.

launch

v. 发起，发动

During the Three Kingdoms period, Lu Kang, a famous general in the late Eastern Wu State, was the son of Lu Xun and the grandson of Sun Ce. In 264 AD, Sun Hao became the emperor of Eastern Wu, and the 38-year-old Lu Kang served as a general.

At that time, the government of Eastern Wu was very corrupt. Sun Hao was a **tyrant**, living a **lewd** life, showing off his military power to the outside world. The number of the army reached one-tenth of the number of the people, the military expense was large, the treasury was empty, and the people had no means to live.

Lu Kang was very dissatisfied with Sun Hao's actions, and repeatedly wrote letters to the emperor, persuading him to strengthen defense externally and improve politics internally to enhance the national power. He once stated

tyrant

n. 暴君

lewd

adj. 荒淫的

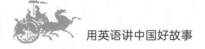

as many as 16 things that should be done in the letter. Sun Hao ignored them all.

In 272, Buchan, who was general of Eastern Wu, surrendered to the Jin State, and Lu Kang led an army to mount a military **expedition**, repelled Jin army, killed the rebel general Bu Chan, and forced Jin State to make peace with Eastern Wu, and then the border area came to a peaceful situation for a while. Sun Hao was very upset about this and sent someone to question Lu Kang, and still wanted to send troops to attack Jin State.

Seeing the continuous deployment of the army and the exhaustion of the people, Lu Kang wrote to Sun Hao, "Now the court is not engaged in causes to enrich the country and strengthen the army, such as stepping up agricultural production, storing food, letting talented people play their roles, so that government offices at all levels do not neglect their duties, strictly enforcing promotion systems to motivate officials, prudently implementing penalties to warn the people, teaching officials with morality, and appeasing the people with kindness. Instead, it let the people who pursue fame to exhaust all their troops and constantly start wars at a great cost and the soldiers are exhausted. In this way, the enemy is not weakened, but we have suffered a serious illness."

Lu Kang also seriously pointed out,"Eastern Wu and Jin State are different in strength. Even if we send troops and win today, it will not be worth the loss. Therefore, we should stop using troops and accumulate strength for

expedition

n. 远征

an opportunity." However, Sun Hao did not listen to Lu Kang's advice. Later, when Lu Kang died, Jin State sent troops to **suppress** Eastern Wu and went down east along the Yangtze River with great force. Eastern Wu was finally destroyed by Jin State.

suppress

v. 镇压

曲高和寡

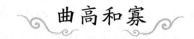

【释义】原比喻知音难得，后用来比喻言论或作品不通俗，不能为多数人所了解或欣赏。

【出处】《对楚王问》："是其曲弥高；其和弥寡。"

  宋玉是战国时楚国著名的文学家，相传是屈原的学生，在楚襄王手下做事。有一次，楚襄王问他："先生最近有行为失检的地方吗？为什么有人对你有许多不好的议论呢？"

  宋玉若无其事地回答说："嗯，是的，有这回事。请大王宽恕我，听我讲个故事：'最近，有位客人来到我们郢都唱歌。他开始唱的，是非常通俗的《下里》和《巴人》，城里跟着他唱的有好几千人。接着，他唱起了还算通俗的《阳阿》和《薤露》，城里跟他唱的要比开始的少多了，但还有好几百人。后来他唱格调比较高难的《阳春》和《白雪》，城里跟他唱的只有几十个人了。最后，他唱出格调高雅的商音、羽音，又夹杂着流利的徵音，城里跟着唱的人更少，只有几个人了。'"

  说到这里，宋玉对楚王说："由此可见，唱的曲子格调越是高雅，能跟着唱的也就越少。圣人有奇伟的思想和表现，所以超出常人。一般人又怎能理解我的所作所为呢？"

  楚王听了，知道是人们误解了宋玉，说："哦，我明白了！"

 成语故事

Difficult Songs Find Few Singers to Join in the Chorus

❖ Paraphrase

It first means that it's hard to find a **bosom friend**, but later it means speeches or works are not popular and cannot be understood or appreciated by most people.

bosom friend

知心朋友

❖ Source

Answers to the Questions of King Chu: It is because the song is difficult that the singers are few.

Song Yu was a well-known writer of Chu State during the Warring States Period. It is said that he was a student of Qu Yuan and worked for King Xiang of Chu. Once, King Xiang of Chu asked him, "Have you misbehaved recently? Why do people have so many bad comments on you?"

Song Yu replied casually, "Well, yes, it is true. Please forgive me and allow me to tell a story: Recently, a guest came to our capital Ying to sing. At first, he sang very popular songs *Xiali* and *Baren*, and thousands of people followed him. Then, he sang fairly popular songs *Yang'a* and *Xielu*, the followers were much less but there were still hundreds of people. Later, he sang more difficult songs *Yangchun* and *Baixue*, and only dozens of people sang with him. Finally, he sang elegant songs in *shang* (musical

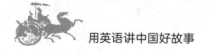

scale), *yu*, mixed with fluent *zhi*, and there were only a few people to follow."

After telling the story, Song Yu said to King Xiang of Chu, "It can be seen that the more elegant the song is, the less the people who can sing it. The saint has extraordinary thoughts and performance, so it is beyond ordinary people. How can ordinary people understand what I do?"

King Xiang of Chu listened and knew that people had misunderstood Song Yu and said, "Oh, I understand!"

人琴俱亡

【释义】 形容看到遗物,怀念死者的悲伤心情,常用来比喻对知己、亲友去世的悼念之情。

【出处】《世说新语·伤逝》:"子敬,子敬,人琴俱亡。"

东晋著名书法家王羲之有七子一女,在书法上都有成就,其中以五子王徽之和七子王献之成就最高。在八个兄弟姐妹中,两人感情最深,王徽之对弟弟非常钦佩,王献之对哥哥也很敬重。

后来,兄弟两人都患了重病,王献之不幸去世了。家人怕王徽之接受不了,就没有把这个消息告诉他。王徽之总是听不到弟弟的消息,很是担心。一天,他实在忍不住,便问家人:"子敬(王献之的字)的病怎样了?为什么好久都没有他的消息?是不是出什么事了?"

家人含糊回答,不敢向他说出实情。王徽之终于明白过来,泣不成声,自言自语地说:"看来子敬已经先我而去了!"

家人知道再也瞒不下去,便说了实话。王徽之听了也不痛哭,只是下了病榻,吩咐仆从准备车辆去奔丧。

到了王献之家,王徽之在灵床上坐了下来。他知道献之生前爱好弹琴,便对献之的家人说:"把子敬的琴取来。"

琴拿来后,王徽之就在灵床上一面弹,一面想着过去兄弟两人的情谊。他越想越悲伤,弹了几次,都不成曲调。于是举起琴向地上掷去,然后叹道:"子敬!子敬!如今人琴俱亡!"

叹罢,悲痛得昏死过去。一个月后,王徽之也离世而去。

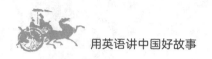

Both the Man and the *Guqin* Are Dead

❖ Paraphrase

It expresses the sadness of seeing the **relic** and missing the deceased. It is often used as a metaphor that the **mourners** miss their deaprted friends or relatives.

relic
n. 遗物

mourner
n. 吊唁者，哀悼者

❖ Source

Grieving for the Departed, A New Account of the Tales of the World: Zijing! Zijing! Now both you and the guqin are dead!

The famous **calligrapher** Wang Xizhi of the Eastern Jin Dynasty had seven sons and one daughter, all of whom had achievements in calligraphy. Among them, the fifth son Wang Huizhi and the seventh son Wang Xianzhi had the highest achievements. Among the eight brothers and sisters, the two have the deepest feelings towards each other. Wang Huizhi admired his younger brother very much, and Wang Xianzhi also respected his elder brother.

calligrapher
n. 书法家

Later, both of the brothers became seriously ill, and Wang Xianzhi passed away unfortunately. The family were afraid that Wang Huizhi could not accept it, so they did not tell him the bad news. Wang Huizhi couldn't hear anything from his younger brother and was very worried. One day, he couldn't help it, and asked his family, "How is Zijing

成语故事

(the courtesy name of Wang Xianzhi)? Why havent't I heard from him for a long time? Is something wrong?"

The family replied vaguely, and were afraid to tell him the truth. Wang Huizhi finally understood, and **chocked** with **sobs**. He said to himself, "It seems that Zijing has already passed away before me!"

The family knew they couldn't hide it anymore, so they told him the truth. Wang Huizhi didn't cry bitterly when he heard it, but got off the bed and ordered his servants to prepare a carriage for the funeral.

When he arrived at Wang Xian's house, Wang Huizhi sat down on the **bier**. Knowing that Xianzhi liked playing the *guqin* when he was alive, he said to Xianzhi's family, "Get Zijing's *guqin*."

After getting the *guqin*, Wang Huizhi played on the bier, thinking about the past with his brother. The more he thought about it, the sadder he became. He played several times, but they were all tuneless. So he lifted the *guqin* and threw it onto the ground, and then sighed, "Zijing! Zijing! Now both you and the *guqin* are dead!"

After this, he fainted with grief. A month later, Wang Huizhi also passed away.

chock

v. 塞满

sob

n. 抽噎

bier

n. 棺材架

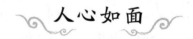

【释义】每个人的思想也像每个人的面貌一样,各不相同。
【出处】《左传·襄公三十一年》:"人心之不同,如其面焉。"

春秋时期,郑国的执政者子皮,想任用年轻的尹何担任大夫,管理自己的封地,当时有很多人反对,认为尹何太年轻,而且没有做官的经验,大家都怕他不能胜任。

子皮不以为然,他认为尹何为人诚实,不会辜负他的期望;也正好让他边干边学,时间长了,就知道怎么治理了。

有位叫子产的大臣,对子皮说:"大王您想培养年轻人当然是件好事,可是这样做反而会害了他。就像叫一个不会用刀的人去切肉,他反而会剁伤自己的手。治理国家也是一样,如果让尹何在正式当大夫之前多加学习,那么,在他从事工作的时候一定会井井有条,否则将会为国家带来想不到的损失。"

子皮听完子产的话,恍然大悟地说:"你说的有道理,以后每件大事我都要事先听听你的意见,才不会犯大错,连我的家事也听从你的意见去做!"

子产摇摇头说:"人心就像人的外貌一样,各不相同,我的意见只能供您参考。我是觉得你让尹何去做大夫有风险,所以据实相告。"

子皮觉得子产对国家非常忠诚,所以把政事完全委托给他。后来,子产把郑国治理得富强起来。

People's Hearts Are like Their Faces

❖ Paraphrase

Everyone's mind is as different as everyone's face.

❖ Source

The Thirty-first Year of Duke Xiang of Lu, Zuo Zhuan: People's hearts are as different as their faces.

During the Spring and Autumn Period, Zi Pi, the ruler of Zheng State, wanted to appoint young Yin He as a scholar-official and manage his fief. At that time, many people were against it, thinking that Yin He was too young and had no experience as an official. Everyone was afraid that he would not be **competent**.

Zi Pi disagreed. He thought Yin He was an honest person and would not let him down. Just let him learn by doing, and at last, he would know how to govern.

A minister called Zi Chan said to Zi Pi, "It is good that Your Majesty want to cultivate young people, but if you do so, it will do harm to him. It's like asking a man who doesn't know how to use a knife to cut meat, and he will cut his own hand instead. The same is true for governing the country. If Yin He can learn more before he officially became a scholar-official, then he will do his work in good order, otherwise it would bring unexpected

competent
adj. 胜任的

losses to the country."

After listening to Zi Chan's words, Zi Pi suddenly said, "What you said makes sense. I will listen to your opinions in advance for every major event in the future, so that I won't make big mistakes. Even for my family affairs I will follow your opinions!"

Zi Chan shook his head and said, "People's hearts are just like their faces. They are different. My opinion can only be used for your reference. I think it is risky for you to let Yin He become a scholar-official, so I just tell the truth."

Zi Pi felt that Zi Chan was very loyal to the country, so he **entrusted** him with political affairs. Later, Zi Chan made Zheng strong and powerful.

entrust

v. 委托，交付

任人唯贤

【释义】用人只选有德有才的人。

【出处】《尚书·咸有一德》:"任官惟贤才,左右惟其人。"

春秋时期,齐襄公有两个弟弟,一个叫公子纠,另一个叫公子小白,他们各有一个很有才能的人来辅佐。由于襄公残暴无道,公元前686年,公子纠跟着辅佐他的管仲到鲁国去避难,公子小白则跟着辅佐他的鲍叔牙逃往莒国。

不久,齐国发生大乱,襄公被杀。齐国大臣派使者到鲁国去迎接公子纠回国当国君,鲁庄公亲自带兵护送。管仲担心公子小白因为离齐国近,而抢先回国夺到君位,就带领一支人马前去拦截,看见公子小白坐在车子里,正往回赶,就偷偷向小白射了一箭。只听小白大叫一声,倒在车里。管仲以为小白死了,马上赶回鲁国。

谁知公子小白并没有死,鲍叔牙将他救治后,抄小路赶到都城,在管仲和公子纠之前回到了齐国,成为国君,就是齐桓公。

不久,管仲和鲁国的军队护送公子纠来到齐国地界,爆发了齐、鲁战争,结果鲁军大败,公子纠被逼死,管仲被抓。齐国的使者表示,管仲射过他们的国君,一定要将他押到齐国去。使者悄悄问管仲:"如果您到齐国后,侥幸没有被杀而得到任用,您将怎么做呢?"

管仲回答道:"要是如你所说,我得到任用,我要任用贤人,使用能人,评赏有功的人。"

管仲被押到齐国都城后,鲍叔牙亲自迎接,齐桓公不仅没有对他报一箭之仇,反而任命他为相国,而鲍叔牙自愿当他的副手。原来,鲍叔牙知道管仲的才能大于自己,所以说服齐桓公这样做。

Appoint People by Their Merits

Paraphrase

Only appoint poeple with morality and talent.

Source

Common Possession of Pure Virtue, Book of Documents: The appointment of officials can only follow the rule to appoint people with both ability and political integrity; the ministers and attendants around the monarch should also be such people.

During the Spring and Autumn Period, Duke Xiang of Qi had two younger brothers, one was called Gongzi Jiu and the other was called Gongzi Xiaobai. They each had a very talented teacher. Because of Duke Xiang's cruelty, in 686 BC, Gongzi Jiu followed his teacher Guan Zhong to seek refuge in Lu State, while Gongzi Xiaobai followed his teacher Bao Shuya to fled to Ju State.

Soon, there was a **turmoil** in Qi State, and Duke Xiang was killed. The minister of Qi State sent envoys to Lu to welcome Gongzi Jiu to return to the country to be the monarch, and Duke Zhuang of Lu State led his troops to **escort** him in person. Gongzi Jiu's master Guan Zhong was worried that Gongzi Xiaobai would return to the country earlier than Gongzi Jiu to seize the throne because he was closer to Qi State, so he led an army to **intercept** Gongzi

turmoil

n. 动乱

escort

v. 护送

intercept

v. 拦截，阻拦

Xiaobai, He saw Xiaobai sitting in the carriage on the way back to Qi State, and he secretly shot an arrow at Xiaobai. He only heard a yell of Xiaobai and saw him fall into the carriage. Guan Zhong thought that Xiaobai was dead, and immediately hurried back to Lu State.

Unexpectedly, Gongzi Xiaobai was not dead. After Bao Shuya rescued him, he rushed to the capital city and returned to Qi State before Guan Zhong and Gongzi Jiu. He became the monarch, Duke Huan of Qi State.

Soon, Guan Zhong and the troops of Lu State escorted Gongzi Jiu to the boundary of Qi State, and the war between Qi State and Lu State broke out. As a result, Lu State was defeated. Gongzi Jiu was forced to death and Guan Zhong was arrested. The envoy of Qi State said that Guan Zhong had shot their monarch and must take him to Qi State. The envoy asked Guan Zhong quietly, "If you were lucky enough to get an appointment after arriving in Qi State instead of being killed, what would you do?"

Guan Zhong replied, "If it is as you said, I will appoint wise and capable people, and reward those who have made contributions."

After Guan Zhong was taken to the capital of Qi State, Bao Shuya greeted him personally. Not only didn't Duke Huan of Qi State take **revenge** on him, but instead appointed him as **premier**, and Bao Shuya volunteered to be his **deputy**. It turned out that Bao Shuya knew that Guan Zhong was more talented than himself, so he persuaded Duke Huan of Qi State to do so.

revenge
n. 报仇
premier
n. 首相
deputy
n. 副手

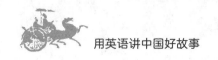

孺子可教

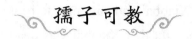

【释义】小孩子是可以教诲的，后形容年轻人有出息，可以造就。
【出处】《史记·留侯世家》："父去里所，复返，曰：'孺子可教矣。'"

　　张良是秦朝末年人，因为行刺秦始皇失败，逃到下邳隐藏起来。

　　有一天，张良在一座桥上遇到一位老人，穿得破破烂烂的。那老人看见张良，把鞋子扔到桥下，对张良说："小伙子，下去把鞋子给我捡上来。"张良下桥把鞋子捡了上来，老人说："给我穿上。"张良跪在地上给他穿上鞋。老人笑着走了。走出老远，又回来对张良说："你这个小伙子可以教啊！五天后的早上到桥上来见我。"

　　五天后一大早，张良就来到桥上，但老人已经先到了。他责备张良来晚了，叫他五天后再来。第二次，鸡一叫张良就赶到桥上，但老人又先到了。这次老人大发脾气，叫他五天后再来。这次，张良半夜就来了，等了一会儿，老人才到。老人非常高兴，送给张良一本书，说："你要下苦功钻研这部书，以后可以做帝王的老师。十年后有大成就。十三年后，你将再见到我，济北谷城山下的黄石就是我啦。"然后，老人就离开不见了。

　　第二天早晨，张良看那本书，乃是《太公兵法》。张良研读《太公兵法》很有成效，成了汉高祖刘邦的重要谋士，为刘邦建立汉朝立下了汗马功劳。

　　十三年后，张良果然在济北谷城山下看到了一块黄色的石头。张良死后，这块石头也埋在了一起。

The Young Man Is Promising

✤ Paraphrase

Children are worth teaching. Later, it means that young people are promising and can be cultivated.

✤ Source

The Hereditary Houses of Liuhou, Records of the Grand Historian: The old man left and then he came back and said , "You are a promising young man! "

Zhang Liang was in the last years of the Qin Dynasty. Because of the failure to **assassinate** Qin Shi Huang, First Emperor of Qin, he fled to Xiapi to hide away.

One day, Zhang Liang met an old man in rags on a bridge. The old man saw Zhang Liang, and he threw the shoes under the bridge, and said to Zhang Liang, "Young man, go down and pick up the shoes for me." Zhang Liang went down the bridge and picked up the shoes. The old man said, "Put on the shoes for me." Zhang Liang knelt on the ground and put the shoes on. The old man smiled and left. After walking far away, he came back and said to Zhang Liang, "You are a promising young man! Come to see me on the bridge in the morning five days later."

Five days later, early in the morning, Zhang Liang went to the bridge, but the old man was already there. He

assassinate

v. 暗杀，行刺

blamed Zhang Liang for being late and told him to come back in five days. The second time, Zhang Liang rushed to the bridge as soon as the cock crowed, but the old man still arrived first. This time the old man **lost his temper** and told him to come back in another five days. This time, Zhang Liang came in the middle of the night, and after a while, the old man arrived. The old man was very happy and gave Zhang Liang a book, saying, "You have to work hard to study this book, and you can be the emperor's teacher in the future. Great achievements will be made in ten years. Thirteen years later, you will see me again, The yellow stone under the Gucheng Mountain in Jibei is me." Then the old man left and disappeared.

The next morning, Zhang Liang read the book, *Tai Gong's Art of War*. Zhang Liang studied the book very effectively and became an important adviser to Liu Bang, Emperor Gaozu of Han Dynasty, and made great contributions to Liu Bang's establishment of the Han Dynasty.

Thirteen years later, Zhang Liang really saw a yellow stone under the Gucheng Mountain in Jibei. After Zhang Liang died, this stone was also buried together with him.

lose one's temper

发脾气，大发雷霆

入木三分

【释义】形容书法极有笔力。现多比喻分析问题很深刻。

【出处】《书断·王羲之》:"王羲之书祝版,工人削之,笔入木三分。"

大书法家王羲之是东晋书法家王旷的儿子。7岁就擅长书法,12岁看见在他父亲枕下有一本书《笔说》,就偷偷读起来。

父亲问王羲之:"你为什么要偷我秘密收藏的书看呢?"

王羲之笑着不回答。母亲问:"你看的是用笔之法吗?"

父亲看他年纪还小,担心不能守住秘密,就告诉王羲之说:"等你长大成人我再教你书法。"

王羲之突然跪了下来,说:"就让孩儿看看这书吧,长大再看就耽误了孩儿幼年的美好才华与发展了。"

父亲听他这么一说,心里很高兴,马上把书给了他。此后不到一个月时间,王羲之的书法就有了很大进步。

有一次,东晋明帝司马绍要到到北郊去祭祀,让王羲之把祝辞写在一块木板上,再派工人雕刻。刻者把木头剔去一层又一层,发现王羲之的墨迹竟渗进木板深处,直到剔去三分厚才见白底!刻者赞叹地说:"这笔力真是入木三分呀!"

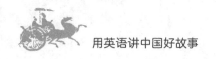

Written in a Forceful Hand

❋ Paraphrase

It means someone's calligraphy is very forceful. Now, it is often used as a metaphor of profound analysis on problems.

❋ Source

Comments on Colligraphy, Wang Xizhi: Wang Xizhi wrote the blessing words on a wooden board and the worker who carved it found the handwriting had **penetrated** deep into the wooden board.

penetrate

v. 渗透

The great calligrapher Wang Xizhi was the son of the Eastern Jin calligrapher Wang Kuang. He was good at calligraphy when he was 7 years old. When he was 12 years old, he saw a book called *On Calligraphy* under his father's pillow and read it secretly.

The father asked Wang Xizhi, "Why did you steal my secret book to read?"

Wang Xizhi smiled and did not answer. The mother asked, "Are you reading the techniques of writing?"

Seeing that he was still young and worried that he would not be able to keep the secret, his father told Wang Xizhi, "I will teach you calligraphy when you grow up."

Wang Xizhi suddenly knelt down and said, "Let me

read this book. If I read it when I grow up, it will be a waste of my talent now and do harm to my progress."

After hearing this, his father was very happy and immediately gave him the book. Less than a month later, Wang Xizhi had made great progress in calligraphy.

Once, the Emperor Sima Shao of the Eastern Jin Dynasty went to the northern **suburbs** to offer sacrifices to ancestors. He asked Wang Xizhi to write the blessing words on a wooden board and then he sent workers to carve it. The carver removed the wood layer by layer, and found that Wang Xizhi's ink had penetrated deep into the wood, and the white background was not visible until a thick layer was removed! The carver said in admiration, "This handwriting is so forceful that it penetrated deep into the wood !"

suburb

n. 郊区

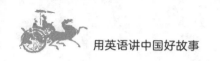

塞翁失马,焉知非福

【释义】比喻一时虽然受到损失,反而因此能得到好处。也指坏事在一定条件下可变为好事,反之亦然。

【出处】《淮南子·人间训》:"马无故亡而入胡,人皆吊之,其父曰:'此何遽不为福乎?'"

古时候,在边塞之地住着一位老人,大家都叫他塞翁。

塞翁家里养了很多马。有一天,他发现少了一匹马。邻居们听说了,都来安慰他,塞翁说:"谢谢大家!丢了一匹马,没准会带来什么好运呢。"大家见塞翁想开了,也就放心了。

果然,过了几天,丢失的马带回来一匹骏马,大家都祝贺他。

塞翁说:"谢谢大家!白白得到一匹马,不一定是什么好事,也许会带来什么麻烦。"

塞翁有个独生儿子,非常喜欢骑马。他发现带回来的马是匹好马,就每天骑着出游,心中得意洋洋,时常策马飞奔。有一次,从马上摔了下来,折断了大腿骨。大家都来安慰他们父子。塞翁说:"谢谢大家!腿摔断了,保住了性命,是不幸中的万幸,怎么就知道不是福气呢?"

过了一年,外敌大举入侵,青年人都应征参战,九成的人都战死了,塞翁的儿子因为腿瘸的原因,没有被招去参战,这样父子俩的性命都保全了。

Sai Weng's Lost of His Horse Maybe a Blessing in Disguise

Paraphrase

It means although you suffer a loss some day, you can get benefits from it later. It also means that bad things can turn into good things under certain conditions, and **vice versa**.

vice versa
反之亦然

Source

In the World of Man, Huainanzi: The horse ran to Hu State for no reason. The neighbors came to comfort him about this. The old man said, "How do you know this is not a good thing?"

In ancient times, there was an old man living in the frontier. Everyone called him Sai Weng.

Sai Weng raised many horses at home. One day, he found that a horse was missing. When the neighbors heard about it, they came to comfort him. Sai Weng said, "Thank you! Losing a horse might bring some good luck." When everyone saw Sai Weng got over it, they were relieved.

As expected, a few days later, the lost horse brought back a fine horse, and everyone congratulated him.

Sai Weng said, "Thank you! Getting a horse for nothing is not necessarily a good thing, and it may cause

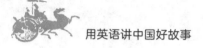

some trouble."

Sai Weng had an only son and he liked riding horses very much. He found that the horse brought back was a good one, so he rode it out every day triumphantly, and often **galloped** around. One day, he fell off the horse and broke his leg. Everyone came to comfort the father and son. Sai Weng said, "Thank you! The leg was broken, but he survived. It is a blessing in misfortune. How do you know that it is not a blessing?"

A year later, foreign enemies invaded the country. All the young people had joined the battle and ninety percent of the young men died in the battle. Sai Weng's son was not **recruited** because of his lameness. In this way, the lives of both father and son were saved.

gallop

v. 骑马奔驰

三顾茅庐

【释义】 比喻真心诚意，一再邀请。
【出处】《前出师表》："三顾臣于草庐之中。"

东汉末年，官渡大战后，曹操打败了刘备。刘备为了实现建国大业，到处搜罗人才。刘备听说隆中的卧龙岗有位叫诸葛亮的隐士，有治国安邦之才，就带上厚礼，和关羽、张飞一起，来请诸葛亮出山，帮自己打天下。他们来到诸葛亮隐居的茅舍，不巧诸葛亮已外出不在家，他们只好打道回府。

过了几天，刘备听说诸葛亮回来了，又和关羽、张飞一起，冒着风雪来到隆中，结果慢了一步，诸葛亮被朋友邀请走了。刘备非常失望，恭恭敬敬地给诸葛亮留下一封信，表明自己对他的景仰和希望他出山的愿望。

转眼到了第二年春天，刘备选择吉日，沐浴更衣，带领关羽、张飞第三次去拜访诸葛亮，诸葛亮正好在家睡觉。他们不让书童去打扰诸葛亮休息，就站在门外等候，直到诸葛亮醒来。

刘备不辞劳苦几次拜访，诸葛亮大为感动，答应做刘备的军师，那年诸葛亮才27岁。

诸葛亮以经天纬地之才辅佐刘备，屡建奇功，最终帮助刘备建立了蜀国，和魏国、吴国成三足鼎立之势。

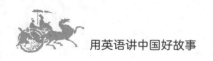

Pay Three Visits to the Hut

Paraphrase

It is a metaphor of a sincere attitude to invite someone repeatedly.

Source

Former Chushibiao: The Late Emperor had visited me for three times in the hut.

At the end of the Eastern Han Dynasty, during the Battle of Guandu, Cao Cao defeated Liu Bei. In order to realize the great cause of founding the nation, Liu Bei looked for talents everywhere. Liu Bei heard that there was a **recluse** named Zhuge Liang in Wolongang, Longzhong, who was talented in ruling the country. So he brought generous gifts with Guan Yu and Zhang Fei to invited Zhuge Liang to help him found a state. They came to the hut where Zhuge Liang lived. Unfortunately, Zhuge Liang was out, so they had to go back.

A few days later, Liu Bei heard that Zhuge Liang was back, and he went to Longzhong with Guan Yu and Zhang Fei in wind and snow. But they were late because Zhuge Liang already went out, invited by a friend. Liu Bei was very disappointed and respectfully left a letter to Zhuge Liang, expressing his admiration for him and the desire to

recluse

n. 隐居者

invite him to be an official.

In the following spring, Liu Bei chose a good day, took a bath and put on clean clothes, and went with Guan Yu and Zhang Fei to visit Zhuge Liang for the third time. Zhuge Liang happened to be sleeping at home. They did not let the servant disturb Zhuge Liang. They just stood outside the door and waited until Zhuge Liang woke up.

Liu Bei **spared no effort** to pay a few visits. Zhuge Liang was very moved and agreed to be Liu Bei's military adviser. Zhuge Liang was only 27 years old that year.

Zhuge Liang assisted Liu Bei with his great talents. He repeatedly made extraordinary achievements, and finally helped Liu Bei establish Shu State, one of the three most powerful states, with Wei State and Wu State, at that time.

spare no effort

不遗余力

三人成虎

【释义】比喻说的人多了，就能使人们把谣言当作事实。

【出处】《战国策·魏策二》："夫市之无虎明矣，然而三人言而成虎。"

战国时期，诸侯国互相讨伐。为了使各国真正遵守盟约，诸侯国之间通常的做法，是以交换太子作为人质。

当时，魏国和赵国签订了友好盟约，照例也要用太子作为人质。为保证太子安全，魏王派大臣庞葱陪同太子前往赵国。庞葱担心自己离开魏国后，会有人借机在魏王面前诬陷他，于是他在临出发前对魏王说："如果有一个人说街市上出现了老虎，大王您相信吗？"魏王回答："我不相信。"

庞葱又问道："如果有两个人说街市上出现了老虎，大王您相信吗？"魏王说："我会有些怀疑。"

庞葱接着说："如果又出现了第三个人说街市上有老虎，大王您相信吗？"魏王回答："我当然会相信。"

庞葱说："很明显，街市上根本不会出现老虎，可是经过三个人的传播，街市上好像就真的有了老虎。而今赵国都城邯郸和魏国都城大梁的距离，要比王宫与街市的距离远很多，对我有非议的人又不止三个，还望大王可以明察秋毫啊。"

魏王说："这个我心里有数，你就放心去吧！"

果然，庞葱刚陪着太子离开，就有人在魏王面前诬陷他。刚开始时，魏王还会为庞葱辩解，诬陷的人多了，魏王竟然信以为真。等庞葱和太子回国后，魏王再也没有召见过他。

Three Men's Talking Makes a Tiger

Paraphrase

It means if there are enough people spreading it, the rumor will turn into a fact in people's minds.

Source

Strategies of Wei II, Strategies of the Warring States: There is no tiger in the street, but when there are three men telling it, people will believe there is a tiger.

During the Warring States Period, **vassal** states started wars against each other. The common practice among vassal states was to exchange princes as hostages in order to make the states truly abide by the agreement of alliance.

At that time, Wei and Zhao signed a friendly agreement, and as a routine, the prince should be exchanged as a hostage. To ensure the safety of the prince, the King of Wei sent minister Pang Cong to accompany the prince to Zhao. Pang Cong was worried that after he left Wei, someone would take the opportunity to **frame** him in front of the King of Wei. So he said to the King of Wei before leaving, "If someone says that there is a tiger in the street, do you believe it?" The king answered, "I won't believe it."

Pang Cong asked again, "If two people say that there is a tiger in the street, do you believe it?" He said, "I will

vassal

n. 属国

frame

v. 作伪证陷害

doubt that a little."

Pang Cong continued, "If there is a third person who says there is a tiger in the street, do you believe it?" He replied, "Of course I will believe it."

Pang Cong said, "It is obvious that a tiger will not appear in the street at all, but after three people spread it, it seems that there really is a tiger in the street. Now the distance between Handan, the capital of Zhao State, and Daliang, the capital of Wei State, is much farther than the distance between the palace and the street. There are more than three people who are against me. I hope that Your Majesty can clearly tell right from wrong."

The King of Wei said, "I know this. You can go **at ease**."

at ease
安心，自在

As expected, as soon as Pang Cong left with the prince, someone framed him in front of the king. At the very beginning, the King of Wei would defend for Pang Cong. But with more and more people coming to say things against him, the king finally believed it. After Pang Cong and the prince returned to Wei, the King of Wei never call him again.

守株待兔

【释义】 比喻不知变通，死守教条；或不经过努力而得到成功的侥幸心理。

【出处】《韩非子·五蠹》："因释其耒而守株，冀复得兔。"

宋国有个农民，他的田地中有一截树桩。

一天，农民正在田里干活，一只跑得飞快的野兔，撞在了树桩上，农民走近一看，兔子已经撞死了。

农民非常高兴，把那只肥肥的兔子拿回家，美美地吃了一顿。

后来农民也不下地干活了，就坐在那个树桩旁边，希望还有别的兔子撞死在树桩上。

一天天过去了，农民再也没有得到第二只兔子，而他田里的庄稼却荒芜了。

这件事一传十，十传百，很快传遍了宋国，人们都取笑他。

Guard a Tree-stump to Wait for Hares

Paraphrase

It is a metaphor of being inflexible and sticking to dogma, or hoping to gain something without paying.

Source

Five Vermin, Hanfeizi: From then on, the farmer abandoned his farming and waited by the stump every day, hoping to get another **hare**.

hare
n. 野兔

There was a farmer in Song State, and there was a stump in his field.

One day, the farmer was working in the field while a running hare directly hit the stump. The farmer walked closer and found that the hare was dead.

The farmer was very happy to take the fat hare home and enjoyed a nice meal.

From then on, the farmer no longer worked in the field, and just sat next to the stump, hoping that another hare would run into the stump and kill itself.

Day by day, the farmer did not get a second hare, and the crops in his fields were lying waste.

The story spread from person to person and soon all over Song State. People all made fun of him.

熟能生巧

【释义】熟练了,就能找到窍门。
【出处】《欧阳文公文集·归田录》:"我亦无他,惟手熟尔。"

宋代有个叫陈尧咨的人,射箭技术极为高超,常因此而骄傲。

他正在给大家表演射箭,箭全射中靶心,于是就向旁边卖油的老人吹嘘起来。

然而老人却说:"没有什么了不起,只不过是手法熟练而已。"说着,拿来一个葫芦,在葫芦口放上一枚铜钱,用勺子舀了一勺油,高高地举起倒了下去。倒下去的油像一条线一样穿过钱眼,全部流进了葫芦,而铜钱上一点油也没沾上。

老人说:"我也没有什么了不起,熟练了,就会掌握窍门,做到出神入化的地步。"

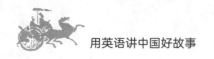

用英语讲中国好故事

Practice Makes Perfect

❖ Paraphrase

If you are experienced in doing something, you will find the tricks in it.

❖ Source

Gui Tian Record, Proses of Ouyang Wengong: I have nothing great either, just being experienced.

In the Song Dynasty, there was a man called Chen Yaozi who was extremely good at shooting and was very proud of it.

One day, he was showing his shooting skills, and all the arrows hit the targets. So he bragged to the old man selling oil next to him.

However, the old man said, "It's nothing great, just an experienced skill." Then, he took a **gourd** and put a copper coin on the mouth of the gourd. Then he **scooped** a spoonful of oil, raised it high and then pour it down. The falling oil passed through the eye of the coin like a thread and all the oil flowed into the gourd, without any on the copper coin.

The old man said, "I have nothing great either. If you are experienced, you will get the tricks, and become a master."

gourd

n. 葫芦

scoop

v. 用勺子舀

揠苗助长

【释义】把禾苗拔高一点,帮它生长。借以比喻违背事物的发展规律,急于求成,反而坏事。也作拔苗助长。

【出处】《孟子·公孙丑上》:"宋人有闵其苗之不长而揠之者,芒芒然归。"

春秋时期,宋国有一个农夫,整日忧心忡忡,担心自己种下的禾苗不长高,天天到田边去看。日复一日,总觉得禾苗一点没有长大。这一天,他忍无可忍,就自己下到田里,将每一颗禾苗都往上拔高一截,一天忙碌下来,筋疲力尽,回到家里对家人说:"今天可把我累坏了,我帮禾苗长高了好多!"他的儿子急忙赶到田边去看,看见被拔起的禾苗都已经枯死了。

想自己的禾苗快快长大是人之常情,但不按照禾苗生长的客观规律办事,一味蛮干,强求速成,就一定会事与愿违。

Pull up Seedlings to Help Them Grow

❖ Paraphrase

Pull the seedlings up to help them grow. It is a metaphor of going against the **law** of things and being eager for success, but only serving as a **hindrance**.

law
v. 规律，法则

hindrance
n. 妨碍，阻挠

❖ Source

Gongsun Chou I, Mencius：There was a farmer of Song who was worried that the seedlings he planted would not grow, so he pulled them all up and went back home exhausted.

During the Spring and Autumn Period, a farmer of Song State was worried all day long that the seedlings he planted would not grow, so he went to the field to check them every day. Day after day, he just felt that the seedlings had not grown up at all. One day, he couldn't wait anymore, so he went down to the field and raised every seedling up a bit. After a busy day, he was exhausted. After he returned home, he said to his family, "Today I am so tired. I helped the seedlings grow a lot." His son hurried to the field and found that the uprooted seedlings had all **withered**.

wither
v. 枯萎，凋谢

It is human nature to expect your seedlings to grow up quickly. But if you don't follow the objective laws, and act

recklessly to pursue a quick success, things will definitely go contrary to your wishes.

recklessly

adv. 不顾一切地

一夫当关，万夫莫开

【释义】一个人把着关口，上万人也打不进来，形容地势十分险峻，便于守御。

【出处】《淮南子·兵略训》："一人守隘，而千人弗敢过也，此谓地势。"

《淮南子》是西汉皇族淮南王刘安及其门客收集史料集体编写而成的一部哲学著作。

刘安生于淮南，汉高祖刘邦之孙，淮南厉王刘长之子。文帝十六年（公元前164年），刘安封淮南王。

《淮南子》在继承先秦道家思想的基础上，糅合了阴阳、墨、法和一部分儒家思想，但主要的宗旨属于道家。胡适说："道家集古代思想的大成，而淮南书又集道家的大成。"

《淮南子·兵略训》认为，用兵有势：气势、因势、地势。将帅充满勇气而蔑视敌人，士兵勇敢而敢于战斗，三军百万，斗志昂扬，气冲霄汉，怒如狂风，吼如雷霆，这叫气势；根据敌方士兵疲劳困倦、松懈混乱、饥饿干渴、寒冷酷暑的情况，乘势动摇敌方的军心，这叫因势；狭窄山路、大河险关、名山大塞，像龙蛇一样盘曲，像竹笠一样起伏，像羊肠一样屈伸，像鱼笱一样险峻，一个人把守要隘，而千万人不能通过，这叫地势。占据了这样的地势，就是取得胜利的绝佳条件。

One Man Can Hold out Against Ten Thousand

❖ Paraphrase

One person guards the pass, and tens of thousands of people can't get in. It is used to describe the **terrain** is very steep and easy to defend.

terrain
n. 地形，地势

❖ Source

On Military Strategy, *Huainanzi*: One person guards the pass, and thousands of people dare not to pass. This is called a good terrain.

Huainanzi is a philosophical work compiled by the Western Han Dynasty royal family King of Huainan, Liu An and his followers by way of collecting historical materials.

Liu An was born in Huainan (now Huainan, Anhui), the grandson of Liu Bang, Emperor Gaozu of Han Dynasty, and the son of Liu Chang, King Li of Huainan. In the 16th year of Emperor Wen (164 BC), Liu An was crowned King of Huainan.

Huainanzi inherited the pre-Qin Taoism and blended *yin* and *yang*, Mohism, Legalism and a part of Confucianism, but its main purpose belongs to Taoism. Hu Shi said, "Taoism gathers the great achievements of ancient

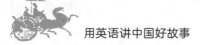

thoughts, and *Huainanzi* gathers the great achievements of Taoism."

According to *On Military Strategy* in *Huainanzi*, a good deployment of troops lies in three factors: morale, situation, and terrain. Generals are full of courage and despise the enemy, and the soldiers are brave and daring to fight. They roar like thunder and rage like storm. This is called the morale. Undermine the spirit of the enemy according to their different states: tiredness, relaxation, disorder, hunger, thirst, cold and heat. This is called making use of the situation. For narrow mountain roads, big rivers, dangerous passes, important mountains and **fortresses**, winding like dragons and snakes, rising and falling like bamboo hats, bending and stretching like sheep's intestines, and as steep as fishhooks, once guarded by one person, thousands of people cannot pass through. This is called the terrain. Occupying such a terrain is an excellent condition for victory.

fortress

n. 要塞

一馈十起

【释义】 吃一顿饭要起来十次。形容事务繁忙。

【出处】《淮南子·氾论训》:"当此之时,一馈而十起,一沐而三捉发,以劳天下之民。"

古时候是禅让制度,就是帝王选择贤良的人来继承自己的位置。尧把帝位禅让给舜,舜又禅让给了大禹。大禹执掌江山后,勤于政事,给自己制造了五件乐器,用来辅助处理公务。

乐器和公务有什么关系呢?原来这五件乐器是鼓、钟、磬、鞀、铎,声音都很洪亮,全部悬挂在大禹的宫殿下。他规定,如有人要给他讲道理,就鸣鼓,鼓声一响,大禹就知道了。要给禹讲大义就撞钟;出事了要报案就击磬;讲述治国之道就敲鞀;如果谁有急事,那么就摇铃铛,也就是铎。

大禹给自己安排了这五件乐器,整天可就忙不过来了。刚端起碗吃饭,外面鼓响了,他赶紧放下碗,出去看看怎么回事。好不容易处理完,回来再吃饭,刚端起碗,那边又敲磬,只好放下碗又马上出来。一顿饭这样起来不下十次,可见大禹勤政爱民的为政态度。

用英语讲中国好故事

Rise Ten Times over a Meal

◆ **Paraphrase**

Rise ten times during a meal, which showed one's diligence in career.

◆ **Source**

A Compendious Essay, Huainanzi: At that time, Yu might be interrupted ten times when having a meal, and might have to hold his wet hair three times to deal with affairs when taking a bath. He worked so hard to serve the people.

In ancient times, it was the **Abdication** System, under which the emperor chose a **virtuous** man to inherit his position. Yao gave the throne to Shun, and Shun gave it to Yu. After taking control of the country, Yu was diligent in political affairs and made five musical instruments for himself to assist in his official duties.

What is the relationship between musical instruments and official duties? It turned out that these five musical instruments were *gu*, *zhong*, *qing*, *tao* and *duo*. Their sounds were very loud and they were all hung under the palace of Yu. He made rules that if someone wanted to reason with him, he could hit the *gu*, and Yu would know it as soon as it banged; if someone wanted to talk about the

abdication
n. 逊位，让位

virtuous
adj. 品德高尚的

the principles of right and wrong, he could ring the *zhong*; if someone wanted to report a case, he could ring the *qing*; if someone wanted to tell the way to govern the country, he could hit the *tao*; if someone had urgent things, then rang the bell, *duo*.

Da Yu made the rules of using five musical instruments for himself, so he was very busy all day long. As soon as he picked up the bowl for a meal, there was a beat of *gu* outside, so he quickly put down the bowl and went out to see what was going on. After having dealt with it, he came back to eat. When he just picked up the bowl, there was a ring of *qing*, so he had to put down the bowl and came out again. He rose more than ten times during a meal, which showed Yu's diligence in politics and his love for the people.

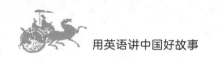

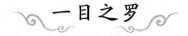

【释义】 只有一个网眼的罗网。比喻只看到一点,而忽视全局。

【出处】《淮南子·说山训》:"今为一目之罗,则无时得鸟矣。"

  有一群鸟飞来了,捕鸟人布了一张大网,结果网到了不少鸟。有个人在旁边仔细观察,发现一个鸟头只钻一个网眼,于是心里就想:何必那么麻烦,把许多网眼结在一起呢?他回到家里,就用一截一截的短绳子,每段结成一个圈,准备也去捕鸟。

  别人问他:"这是做什么用的?"

  他回答说:"去捕鸟用的。反正一只鸟头只钻一个洞,我这种绳子圈成的网眼岂不比一张大网省事多了么?"

  捕鸟用的网固然是由一个个网眼构成,但如果离开了整张网,靠单个的网眼是肯定捕不到鸟的。

A One-mesh Net

❖ Paraphrase

A net with only one **mesh**. It is a metaphor for people who can only see one point, but ignore the overall situation.

mesh

n. 网孔，筛孔

❖ Source

Discourse on Mountains, Huainanzi: Now the net has only one mesh, and no bird will be caught.

A flock of birds came, and the birdcatcher cast a big net. As a result, many birds were caught. A man was watching carefully and found that a bird's head **popped out** of only one mesh, so he thought to himself, "Why bother to tie so many meshes together?" When he returned home, he used short pieces of ropes to tie a small circle on each, preparing to catch birds too.

pop out

突然伸出

Someone asked him, "What is this for?"

He replied, "I use it to catch birds. Anyway, a bird's head only pops out of one mesh. Won't my one-mesh nets save a lot trouble than a big net?"

The net for catching birds is indeed made up of individual meshes, but without the whole net, no bird can be caught by a single mesh.

朝三暮四

【释义】原比喻聪明人善于使用手段,愚笨的人不善于辨别事情,后来比喻反复无常。

【出处】《庄子·齐物论》:"狙公赋芧曰:'朝三而莫(暮)四。'众狙皆怒。"

从前,宋国有一个老人,很喜欢猴子,家里养了一大群猴子。时间长了,他能了解猴子的脾气秉性,猴子也能听懂他说的话。老人愈发喜欢它们了,宁愿减少全家的口粮,也要让猴子吃饱。

由于猴子多,消耗大增,老人家里的存粮一天比一天少了。没有办法,他只好限定猴子的食物数量,就向猴群宣布:"从今天早饭起,你们吃的橡树果实要定量,早上三个,晚上四个,怎么样,够了吧?"

猴子听了,一个个龇牙咧嘴,乱蹦乱跳,没把老人的话当回事。老人知道猴群生气了,就重新宣布:"既然你们嫌少了,那就早上四个,晚上三个,这样可以了吗?"

猴群听说早上从三个增加到四个,都以为增加了食物,一个个围过来,摇头摆尾,伏在老人周围,咧着大嘴直乐呵。

Three in the Morning and Four in the Evening

✤ Paraphrase

It is originally a metaphor that smart people are good at playing tricks and stupid people are not good at telling right from wrong. Later it is a metaphor of changing one's mind frequently.

✤ Source

On the Equality of Things, Zhuangzi: The owner of the monkeys said, "Three in the morning, and four in the evening." The monkeys were all angry.

Once upon a time, there was an old man in Song State who liked monkeys very much and raised a large group of monkeys at home. After a long time, he could understand the temper of the monkeys, and the monkeys could also understand what he said. The old man became more and more fond of the monkeys, and would rather reduce the family's food to feed the monkeys.

Due to the large number of monkeys, the food in the old man's home was getting less and less day by day. He had no choice but to limit the amount of food for the monkeys. He announced to the monkeys, "From the breakfast this morning, the **acorns** you eat will be limited.

acorn
n. 橡子，橡实

Three in the morning and four in the evening. How about it? Is that enough?"

The monkeys showed their teeth and jumped, not taking the old man's words seriously. Knowing that the monkeys were angry, the old man again announced, "Since you think the food is not enough, then four in the morning and three in the evening. Is that all right?"

Hearing that the number had increased from three to four in the morning, the monkeys all thought that their food had been increased. They came to the old man one by one, shaking their heads and tails, leaning close to him and kept **grinning**.

grin

v. 咧嘴笑

自相矛盾

【释义】 比喻言行不一或互相抵触。

【出处】《韩非子·难一》:"以子之矛陷子之盾,何如?"

战国时期,有个楚国商人,在市场出售自制的长矛和盾牌。

他先把盾举起来,夸耀说:"我卖的盾牌是最坚硬的,无论用多么锋利的长矛,也别想刺透我的盾牌。"

然后,他又举起长矛,夸耀说:"我卖的长矛是最锋利的,无论多么坚硬的盾牌,我的长矛一刺就穿。"

现场有人问他:"如果用你的长矛去刺你的盾牌,是刺得穿还是刺不穿呢?"

楚国商人涨红了脸,半天回答不上来。

Spear and Shield

Paraphrase

It means one's words and deeds are not matched or **contradictory**.

contradictory
adj. 相互矛盾的

Source

Series One of Criticisms of The Ancients, Han Feizi: If you stab your shield with your spear, what will happen?

During the Warring States Period, there was a businessman of Chu State who sold his self-made spears and shields in the market.

He raised the shield first and boasted, "The shield I sell is the hardest. No matter how sharp a spear is, it won't pierce my shield."

Then he raised his spear, boasting, "The spear I sell is the sharpest. No matter how hard a shield is, my spear will pierce it."

Someone asked him, "If you use your spear to stab your shield, will it be pierced or not?"

The businessman of Chu State **blushed** and couldn't answer the question for a long time.

blush
v. 脸红，涨红了脸